Blitzed City

A Birmingham Childhood

Muriel Bolton

DEDICATION

To Annie and Bill who survived the Blitz and gave my
sisters and me a secure and love-filled home
in spite of shortages and hard times.
To Colin who has patiently read and corrected copies
of this story and made endless cups of tea.
To our children, Mark, Clare and Jane and our
grandchildren who will read it and marvel at how
primitive things were in the 'Olden Days.'

CONTENTS

1 What a Difference a Day Made   Pg 1

2 The Eagle Stirs   Pg 4

3 The Phoney War   Pg 11

4 Shattered Dreams   Pg 21

5 Dunkirk   Pg 26

6 At Home in Church Street   Pg 30

7 The Birmingham Blitz   Pg 35

8 November 22—Fire Storms   Pg 43

9 Blitz Christmas 1940   Pg 48

10 The Night of a Thousand Fires   Pg 53

11 A Port in the Storm   Pg 57

12 Bayswater Road   Pg 62

13 Hard Times   Pg 71

14 The Great British Train   Pg 78

15 Wartime Christmas   Pg 82

16 Hospitals and Holidays   Pg 89

17 Hollyhocks and Handstands   Pg 93

18 A New School 1944   Pg 101

19 D—Day 1944   Pg 107

20 Bells Ring…Flags Fly   Pg 110

21 Advance Britannia   Pg 114

22 General Election…Labour Victory   Pg 118

23 The Big Freeze 1947   Pg 124

24 Diverging Plans   Pg 129

25 The Dell   Pg 135

26 November…Fogs and a Wedding   Pg 140

27 Grammar School   Pg 143

28 Youth Club   Pg 148

29 I am a Teenager   Pg 153

30 O Dear…O Levels   Pg 160

31 Dunster Beach in the 1950s   Pg 163

32 In the Footsteps of Florence   Pg 167

33 My First Ward   Pg 172

34 At Last I Carry a Lamp   Pg 170

35 Call *this* Midwife   Pg 189

36 Sailing Away on the Queen Elizabeth Pg 193

37 Mississippi Summer Night's Dream   Pg 198

38 Back Home to Birmingham   Pg 204

WHAT A DIFFERENCE A DAY MADE

Church bells rang across Britain. From every town and hamlet, bells rang loud and clear, breaking the silence of six years.

In my hometown of Birmingham, bunting went up in spite of drizzling rain. Forgotten Union Jacks were unearthed from attics and cupboards; bright splashes of colour draped windows and trees. Tables stretched along the green opposite our house. Dozens of tables loaded with food that miraculously appeared in spite of rationing. A woodpile for the bonfire grew steadily. By the afternoon, it towered over me; I stared at the chair on top, however did it get up there? The entire neighbourhood gathered, mums, dads, children, friends and families. Adults lounged and chatted, children played through long fun-filled hours; egg and spoon races, sack races and every conceivable game.

And still the bells rang. Hour after hour of joyful peals throughout that long, unforgettable day. Darkness fell, and the gigantic bonfire was lit. For the first time, I saw fireworks; I held my breath as they crackled and fizzed and rockets whooshed with bursts of stars, into the inky sky. I fizzed with excitement too. In fact, I couldn't keep still. I hopped, skipped and jumped on my eight-year-old legs from one group to another, from one activity to another. I was desperate to know what everyone was doing. The flames of the fire leapt higher and higher, and the smell of wood-smoke drifted on the night air.

After years of darkness, lights were on all over Britain. Street lights glowed and lights twinkled from the doors and windows of myriads of homes.

For more than five relentless years, Nazi planes, with their payload of bombs, had tried to find British cities. Land and sea merged and looked the same in the brooding, 'blacked out' darkness. Fifty million people were hidden under that black shroud.

Where were they?

But this was the day the lights went on again. From coast to coast Britain blazed with light. The aerial view must have been fantastic. What a difference a day made!

Black curtains were tossed onto bonfires. Joy and excitement mounted as reality dawned; it was over; it truly was over. I watched the adults jitterbug and jive to improvised music, and then we all made a long, long, very long, 'crocodile' and danced down the road doing the 'conga.' Everybody shouted 'aye-aye-conga.' Then, there was a circle to dance an energetic hokey-cokey. Arms went up in the air, the song got louder as everyone rushed to the centre singing, 'Oh the hokey-cokey.' I didn't know what it meant, but I joined in the unforgettable fun. This was partying in a way I have never seen since.

The fire burned low, and out came old chairs, tables, benches—anything that would burn. We children stayed up long after bedtime. Gradually, we dropped to sleep around the fire to the sound of singing that went on through the night. 'We'll meet again, don't know where don't know when, but I know we'll meet again some sunny day'–'There'll always be an England'–'There'll be bluebirds over the white cliffs of Dover'–'Roll out the barrel; we'll have a barrel of fun.'

And we really did have a barrel of fun.

More wood for the fire, more singing and dancing, more laughter and joy, we thought it would go on forever. When the fire died down to a glowing circle, potatoes were buried in the embers. They were as black as charcoal when they came out, but tasted so good.

We sat around the fire, a big neighbourhood family, tired, drowsy and happy. The silly jokes started. Then there were hysterical giggles, and then more singing. 'If you were the only girl in the world'. . .'Daisy, daisy, give me your answer do.' My favourite, 'Run rabbit, run, run, don't give the farmer his fun, fun, fun', became 'Run Adolph, run Adolph, run, run, run.' But 'Why Adolph?' I wondered. It was 3 or 4am when Mum and Dad finally carried us over the road to bed.

I didn't realise that we were making living history—actors in stories that would be told for years to come. *We were celebrating the end of the war.* A war that began five years, eight months and four days before, when I was two years old. . .

THE EAGLE STIRS

At 11am on Sunday 3 September, 1939, the Prime Minister Neville Chamberlain, told the nation that Britain and France were at war with Germany. His announcement brought to a head the uncertainty of the last few years. There had been an uneasy tension in Europe, the German Eagle under Nazi Adolph Hitler, was stirring and making ominous sounds of war.

At home, Britain was coming to terms with an abdication and a new King. Edward VIII gave up the throne, after only eight months, to marry the American divorcee Wallis Simpson. His brother George was crowned King in May 1937. Hesitatingly, Britain celebrated the new reign as war clouds increased.

When it came, the announcement of war was not a surprise. In the previous year, Germany had built up her naval and armed forces. German troops had already annexed Austria and invaded Czechoslovakia, and although Hitler signed a peace agreement with Neville Chamberlain over Poland; he was clearly not intending to honour it.

Hoping for the best but preparing for the worst; Britain also prepared for war. Gradually, during that hot sultry summer of 1939, hopes of peace faded. The nation was alerted that something was imminent when the terse order, *'Evacuate children immediately'* came on Thursday, 31 August. On Friday, children arrived at railway stations in every city across the country as evacuation plans were implemented. By Saturday, streets and homes were strangely silent. The laughter and shouts of thousands of children were missing. The full horror began to dawn.

My parents, Annie and Bill Johnson, waited for news. *Where there is dialogue between my parents, and I refer to them as Annie and Bill, I relate what they later told me in many conversations, but I also include the sort of things they probably said.* Where I refer to them as Mum and Dad, those are actual memories.

For four tense days, during that long weekend, Annie and Bill waited. The whole nation waited for the confirmation of war that they knew would come. Hour after hour they listened to the wireless or rushed to buy newspapers. The BBC gave regular news bulletins and reported that Winston Churchill had been invited to join a War Cabinet. The weekend dragged on.

'I wonder if Mary's all right.'

Bill was sitting at the big oak table whilst Annie cooked breakfast. In the background the wireless alternated music and news on that sunny Sunday morning in September. Alexander's Ragtime Band, was followed by Bob Hope singing thanks for the memory. The waiting seemed endless.

Annie shook her head; she was near to tears as she spread a clean cloth on the table and put three teaspoons of loose tea into the teapot. One for Bill, one for Annie and one for the pot. She covered the pot with a knitted tea-cosy reminiscent of a lady's ball gown. Prising the metal top off a bottle, she poured Birmingham sterilised milk into a jug.

'She was crying when I left her.'

They had talked all night about Mary's evacuation, Bill didn't know what else to say. He poured a cup of tea and heaped several spoons of sugar into the liquid. 'Tea is always the answer', he thought, as he watched Annie fry the bacon and then add his favourite oat cakes into the hot fat. It was always bacon on Sunday, He had no appetite today.

'I'll fetch her back', Annie finally said. 'We'll look for a house further out of the city.'

'So will hundreds of others, if only we had moved before.'

They were so disappointed. That very weekend, their long-held plans for buying their own home had been dashed. All summer they watched as new houses were built on Cherry Orchard Farm at the edge of Handsworth. They helped Bill's sister Kath, move into hers, and waited for their turn. Annie and Bill were country folk and the houses, further out of Birmingham next to open fields, were perfect. But yesterday they learned that all building projects were stopped and materials were to be diverted to the war effort.

Bill tried to change the subject, 'Where's my little girl?'

'Here I am,' I ran to him and he picked me up. Dad's knee, was a safe place.

Annie looked at Bill sitting opposite her. He was totally devoted to her. Mothers with small children, were offered evacuation to a safe place but Annie refused. If she went away, she would have to leave Bill and wouldn't be with Mary, if she stayed with Bill she would be without Mary anyway. Now the family was divided. Annie's tears erupted again.

Five-year-old Mary had just started at tiny St Silas school when Annie was called in to talk about evacuation. It was the hardest decision she and Bill had ever made. She shuddered at the memory of blaring loudspeaker vans touring the streets shouting, 'Evacuate immediately.' The next day Annie took Mary to the school around the corner. She was dressed in warm clothes, with a name label on her coat and carrying her gas mask in a little cardboard box and a bag with spare clothes. The two small rooms of the school were filled with mothers and children and many were crying. It was terrible leaving her there and now they didn't even know where she was staying.

They sat in silence for a long time, just waiting. Outside, the sun was warm and bright and church bells were beginning to ring.

A lovely, normal Sunday morning. But it wasn't normal.

Bill eventually said, 'I think I'll go and work on the shelter; I'm going to make bunk beds for the girls, I think we will be safe in it.'

Anxiety gripped him as he worked on the bunks. He remembered the terrible things that happened in the First World War. It was happening again and here he was, building a shelter to protect his family from bombs. Another wave of anxiety made him clutch his stomach. He often had terrible stomach pains when anxious. He'd been in hospital with a perforated stomach ulcer before, he couldn't be ill now with three small children to look after. Would a shelter protect them? It would be terrible to lose his girls in a raid. He tried to get on with the bunks but couldn't concentrate.

The shelter was at the bottom of the garden. He had worked on it for several weeks and now there were only bunks to make. 'I think I'll fix a line from the back door along the path to the shelter,' he thought, 'that will give us something to hold onto in the dark.'

The shelter was formed from two corrugated iron sheets joined at the top to form an arch, it had a wall at the back and a sand-bagged door at the front. The sides were sunk four feet into the ground and camouflaged with two feet of soil on top, then grass or plants. They were named after Lord Anderson, who was responsible for Civil Defence, and a 100 thousand were built in Birmingham. They could withstand five hundred pounds of High Explosive bomb exploding within a few yards and saved many lives during the war.

Several months before the war, Mum wrote to her Father in Australia and said that the Corporation were going from house to house to check who was entitled to an Anderson shelter. She said, 'Anyone earning under £250 per year, plus an allowance of £50 for each child is entitled to a free shelter. That means we can have a free one, otherwise it would cost £8-10s.' I think Dad was earning £5 a week which was a good wage for the time, but the child allowance for three children had brought us down into the free entitlement range.

Bill tried to get on but couldn't concentrate. His thoughts went to the time when their first baby died of meningitis. Cathleen was a year old and Annie was heartbroken. It took a long time to recover but it was even worse when Peter died.

Peter was a cherub with fair hair and blue eyes; they were so proud of him. Already a chattering toddler, he was two when he caught a cold and pneumonia followed. Annie and Bill watched over his cot for days as he became desperately ill. Annie wept, these were the days before antibiotics. Bill wept as he carried another tiny coffin to the grave where Peter was buried with his sister. Annie was inconsolable. And now they were parted from Mary.

Bill's thoughts were interrupted by Annie, 'Come quickly, there's going to be an announcement.'

The news they awaited was finally broadcast at 11am. Neville Chamberlain, in an expressionless voice, explained that Hitler had invaded Poland and that Britain was committed to protecting Poland. A deadline to withdraw had been given but Hitler had not responded. Consequently, he said, 'Britain and France are now at war with Germany.' It was Sunday 3 September, 1939. Across the continent, Polish people in Warsaw sang 'God Save the King' and cheering crowds outside the British Embassy shouted,

'Long live Britain.'

Annie and Bill sat in silence, heaviness enveloping them. Finally, Annie true to form, said 'We'll manage as long as we're together.'

'We will,' Bill gripped his stomach and winced. He needed to be well enough for work tomorrow.

He sat down at the little organ and began pumping the pedals. And then he sang, in his lovely deep voice, 'Bless this house O Lord we pray, keep it safe by night and day, bless these walls so firm and stout, keeping want and trouble out.' It was a favourite of his and he was often heard singing those lines as they went through the traumas of war.

Bill's mind went to the events of the last few days. The alert to evacuate children came on Thursday 31 August, two days before war was officially announced. Loudspeaker vans toured the streets, blaring out instructions for children to report to their schools the next day for evacuation. 'Evacuate immediately.' How primitive but how effective. Every mother hearing that, must have hurried home fearful but ready to respond.

The Birmingham Post carried information about the evacuation on Friday 1 September. The announcement read, 'One hundred special trains have been chartered to transport 90 thousand children from the three city stations. Trains will leave throughout the day between 8am and 5pm.'

Parents were asked not to go to the station to see their children off but to take them to school. An urgent appeal was made to all available St John's ambulance men to assist. In addition to school children and mothers with young children, the newspaper reported that there would also be a partial evacuation of twelve Birmingham hospitals to make precautionary provision for war casualties. An emergency hospital was to be opened in the basement of Lewis' Department store to deal with central area casualties.

The Chief of the Auxiliary Fire service reported, 'Every station is manned and we are in a fully organised state.'

In a message to the City, the Lord Mayor of Birmingham said, 'The time has come; I am confident citizens will take careful consideration of directions for safety over the wireless. Birmingham is ready to meet any aggressive movement with determination and calmness.'

Annie and Bill realised their worst fears had materialised; empty schools, hospitals in department stores, shelters, and rationing. But they knew the battle of this war would be over home ground and the air raids were expected to be far worse than those of the First World War. They shared the fears of the nation; there was no escape.

On 3 September Neville Chamberlain set up a war cabinet and invited Winston Churchill to become First Lord of the Admiralty. A year later Chamberlain resigned and Winston became Prime Minister and led the country through the war years.

From 3 September, church bells across the country were silent. Communication was basic, and it was agreed that in the event of an invasion, the bells would be the obvious and easiest way to inform the population. *The joyful sound of bells, carried on the air, across every community, was no longer part of the British Sunday scene.* Again it seems primitive, but news was limited to newspapers, wireless, telegrams and cinemas.

These plans were not hastily put together but had been in preparation for several years. Birmingham was prepared. An Evening Despatch reporter wrote after the war, 'Long before the raids started, Birmingham was ready as far as any city could have been ready. It was mentally stripped for action against the unimaginable.'

The consequences of the declaration of war were swift. On September 11, the Ministry of Information released the news that a British Expeditionary Force had successfully landed in France to co-operate with the French Army. The operation took place over several days and a Daily Mail reporter said it happened so secretly that few knew they had gone. The troopships crossed at dead of night escorted by naval boats, passenger liners, cross-channel ferries and each were painted a dark battleship grey. 'The Tommies came from bases in all parts of the country and crossed in good spirits singing and whistling the old songs of twenty-five years ago … Tipperary … Pack up your Troubles in your Old Kit Bag and Keep the Home Fires burning.' The British Force was established in 1938 in readiness and 158,000 troops were transported within nine days of the declaration of war on September 3.

So it was war … Bill thought about the sad years he and Annie had been through before they came to Birmingham for a better life. He thought about Talke Pits in Staffordshire where both had deep roots going back many generations. His mind went over the hard times they experienced there. He thought about Annie's heartbreak when her parents emigrated to Australia leaving her behind, because she wanted to marry Bill. She still grieved the loss of her large and happy family. He thought of the strikes and unemployment of the 1920s and the devastating loss of their first two babies. He thought of Mary somewhere in the country. She would be safe but what if she was left an orphan? He thought of his own father who died when he was eight leaving him the oldest child to support a widowed mother. *So many losses.* Bill thought about the better life they thought had started when they came to Birmingham in 1936.

It would be another year before the first air-raids began on cities across Britain. From August 1940, the wail of sirens and the drone of German planes were heard night after night over our home in Church Street. Birmingham's large number of factories, producing planes and ammunition, made it a key target. During the blitz of 1940, more than five thousand High Explosive bombs were dropped on Birmingham in seventy-seven air raids; as well as thousands of incendiary bombs, which set the city ablaze again and again. Our home in Church Street Lozells was right at the centre of those raids.

One of my earliest memories is of standing on the garden path with my mother. 'Dad is on fire watch in that factory', she said, pointing to flames that were leaping towards the sky. The sky glowed from horizon to horizon. Brilliant reds and oranges fused together with black smoke. In the middle of the night, it was as light as day. That sky, with the amazing rainbow of colours, is deeply etched into my memory. There were sounds of explosions, searchlights sweeping the sky, and formations of advancing planes. I stared fascinated; the city blazed but to my young eyes it seemed exciting.

I was three-and-a-half and for a child who is daily experiencing new events, even the extraordinary is normal. It didn't seem strange to see bombs falling out of the sky, to sleep in shelters or live with rationing and blackout. I just assumed that was the way life was. I am not aware of what my mother was feeling. We stood for a long time watching the fire until she took me back into the shelter. How could Dad survive that blaze? She must have thought that she might be widowed and left alone with three small children.

3

THE PHONEY WAR

The waiting year was often called the *phoney war.* War was first fought on land on the continent as Germany invaded one country after another. On 29 Sept 1939, every home in the country was visited and the personal details of every civilian recorded on a National Registration role. This was used to identify who was available for national service, who for munitions work and who was allowed to stay at home to look after pre-school children. From this, a list was drawn up of occupations exempted from call-up—farmers, miners, bakers, grocers, railway workers, teachers and essential service providers. Identity cards were issued on the spot and were to be carried at all times. This role was also used to co-ordinate rationing.

Those records have just been released and Bill was recorded as an Electrical and Mechanical Engineer and Annie as having 'unpaid domestic duties.' Children were also recorded but the names of any still alive are *blacked out.* There are only two blacked out names at number 7 Church Street, those of Ann and myself. Mary had been evacuated on 3 September so was not there.

Bill was thirty-seven and exempt from military service because of his age and his health. He had a stomach ulcer which had already perforated twice. In addition to his daytime work he took on shift duties as a night-time fire warden. This was compulsory for men at home.

According to newspapers, the winter of 1939 to 1940 was bitterly cold. December and then January brought frequent frosts and heavy snowfalls with temperatures well below zero. Biting east winds seemed to whip through even the heaviest of clothes. Newspapers reported that ice covered many rivers and the Thames was frozen for eight miles. In Birmingham, the

Grand Union Canal was completely frozen over and closed to essential transporting of coal and war supplies by barge. This was serious.

As 1939 ended and the daylight shortened, blackout added to the daily misery. From the day war was declared, and long before the first bombing raids, street lighting was turned off across Britain. Every house was required to put up blackout curtains. The slightest light could alert enemy planes to where cities and homes were. The streets were patrolled at night by wardens and occasionally, 'Put that light out' or 'close that curtain,' could be heard. One wartime leaflet advised householders that five-watt light bulbs were perfectly adequate!

I have a flash memory of hearing a lot of noise in the street and going outside with Mum and Dad. A chimney was on fire; flames were blazing up into the darkness. A crowd of neighbours were shouting angrily, 'Put that fire out.' A chimney fire was a real fear. Fuel wasn't smokeless in those days and soot could build up in chimneys and spontaneously catch fire. Flames blazing from a chimney would draw the attention of enemy planes.

Blackout times were published in local papers and there were heavy fines for breaking the rules. It is impossible to imagine the total darkness, when not a single street or house light can be seen; yet people still had to move around. There were many accidents and even locals were confused and got lost. To add to the difficulties, road signs and directions were removed or reversed to confuse the enemy in the event of an invasion.

Air Raid Precaution Schemes had been established for several years and were in place nationwide in the event of aerial attack by Germany. The ARP for Birmingham covered many areas and was co-ordinated from a basement in the Council House in the City centre in Victoria Square. From here it was in constant contact with six other ARP outposts around the City so that raids could be plotted as they happened and resources deployed.

Across the country, barrage balloons, looking like huge, grey flying elephants were in place around cities in an attempt to hinder low flying German planes and thousands of air raid shelters were already built. Stirrup pumps were distributed in the event of fire. These consisted of a pump placed into a bucket of water, a handle to pump up and down and a length of hose to spray water. Houses with pumps were marked with a white 'S' painted on the wall outside. To see one in action is to wonder just how effective they could be!

Civil Defence leaflets advising on blackout and protection of the home had been distributed to every household and gas masks given to each man woman and child in the country. Instructions were. *'Carry your gas mask at all times.'* If a warden or policeman was heard shouting, 'Gas, gas, gas,' they were to be put on immediately. Warnings were as primitive as that. . .a man on a bike shouting, 'Gas.' Gas masks looked frightening to children and they were given Mickey Mouse masks, to alleviate the fears and Mickey became a hero in many homes.

The evacuation of children had been planned for years and in July 1939, the Government published a leaflet called 'Evacuation, How and Why.' It explained that in the event of war, big cities might be subjected to determined attacks from the air and the Government had made plans for the removal of school children to safer places. Birmingham was a target city because of the large numbers of factories that could be turned to producing munitions. During the summer of 1939 parents were called into schools to discuss evacuation procedures.

Operation Pied Piper moved millions of children nationwide, and involved advance planning for teachers, workers, helpers, railways and host homes. It was before the days of computers, TV, mobile phones or even phones in every home and yet it worked. The scheme was voluntary but information leaflets said children would be safer and happier away from the cities. They would have their school teachers with them and schooling would be continued. It was not possible to let parents know in advance the place to which each child would be sent but they would be notified as soon as the movement was over.

A list was given of what each child should take with them which included gas mask, a change of underclothing, night-clothes, house-shoes or plimsolls, spare socks, a toothbrush, comb, towel and handkerchiefs, a warm coat or mackintosh, and a packet of food for the day. Meanwhile, those who were able to take evacuees were told it was their public duty, part of the war effort, to take children from cities. Hosts would receive 8s 6d for each child accommodated.

Birmingham, the 'City of a Thousand Trades', diverted its many factories to producing munitions and by the end of the war 400,000 were employed in war work. Writer and author, Carl Chinn, in 'Brum Undaunted' makes a long list of these diversions, for instance—Samuel Heath's brass bedstead business turned to making blow lamps, paraffin stoves, firing pins and primers. Bournville Utilities, of Cadbury's Chocolates, employed 2,000 people who made machine tools, lathes, milling machines, aero parts, anti-aircraft rockets and respirators.

Another interesting diversion was Chad Valley Toys made in Harborne. They changed to making gun cases, hospital tables, tent poles and *board games and jigsaws for the military forces.* Chad Valley was started by Alfred Johnson in the 1800s and was a family firm for many years. It originally made soft toys and especially Teddy Bears. In 1945 the company returned to toy production and expanded to include decorated tin cars, tin boxes and domestic hardware. Every Birmingham child grew up knowing about Chad Valley Toys.

Apart from extra workers for these factories, there was a call for fire wardens, fire watchers, fire fighters, ambulance drivers, first aid workers and staff for feeding centres for the homeless. Many of these were voluntary and worked long hours after a day-time job. The St John's Ambulance and WVS workers also gave tireless and invaluable service.

One evening just before Christmas 1939, Bill walked slowly and carefully home from work. It was 6:30pm and not the tiniest chink of light showed from any window. It was hard going. He turned his torch on from time to time to see where he was.

'It's a good job the kerbs are painted white', he thought, 'I can hardly see where to go.'

Three hundred and fifty miles of Birmingham kerbs were painted to help night-time journeys; housewives were urged to paint those outside their own homes.

Finally, he turned into Church Street and then into number seven, took off his trilby and hung it with his coat in the hall. It was bitterly cold outside and wasn't much warmer inside the hall. Coal was rationed and the only source of heating was the fire in the back room; but that room was light and warm from the small fire and from the gas stove cooking his dinner. It smelled good.

He sat at the table and warmed his hands on the hot cup of tea which Annie gave him.

'I'm glad to be home, it's so slippery and it's going to snow, that'll make travelling even worse.' It was Friday and Bill put his pay packet on the table.

'We'll have to tighten our belts; tax has gone up to 7s and 6d in the pound.'

The increase from 5s, was to pay for the cost of the war and everyone was affected. Bill earned a good wage, but the extra would be difficult to absorb.

'That's nearly a fifty per cent increase,' said Annie, wondering how she was going to manage, food was getting so expensive. 'On top of that, the ration books arrived today; cheese, butter, sugar and bacon are rationed and we are only allowed one egg each a week.'

'We're going to be short of food as well as money.' Bill's heart sank as he remembered the last war and the hardships and years of unemployment. 'But Kath said she'd let us have five eggs a week when her hens are laying.'

'Well, at least Mary's back home', Annie frowned, 'even though she hasn't been to school for two months.'

Evacuation wasn't compulsory but 'Evacuation with teachers,' was the 'City Policy,' and there would be no schooling for those who stayed behind. Mary was evacuated but was terribly unhappy away from home. She cried continually, she was scared of barking farm dogs and was stung by a bee. Finally, after four weeks, the host family wrote and asked Annie to fetch her home. And so Mary returned along with a steady stream of children from around the country. Two hundred schools in central areas of Birmingham had been closed since September.

Birmingham Corporation wasn't prepared for the rate at which children came back. It was a huge problem. Some children remained in the country with teachers, whilst others returned and were without schooling. It is thought that up to forty thousand Birmingham children were without education in the first months of the war. Schools remained closed until shelters were built in playgrounds.

Bill picked up the Birmingham Mail. It cost 1d, but it was one of the few ways of getting news, the wireless was so unreliable, he didn't want to give up the Mail even if things were tight. He didn't expect to read good news, just reminders about blackout, reminders about carrying identity cards, reminders that children were best off evacuated to the country.

On Christmas Day, at 3pm, King George broadcast his Christmas message live from Sandringham. Many tuned in to listen as he said, 'A New Year is at hand we cannot tell what it will bring. If it brings peace, how thankful we shall all be. If it brings us continued struggle, we shall remain undaunted.'

The King finished by quoting from a poem that would be remembered as a message of encouragement and re-assurance in the dark times of war.

And I said to the man who stood at the gate of the year: "Give me a light that I may tread safely into the unknown."

And he replied: "Go out into the darkness and put your hand into the Hand of God. That shall be to you better than light and safer than a known way." So I went forth, and finding the Hand of God, trod gladly into the night.

It was 1939 and the following Christmas was at the height of the Blitz.

The waiting year was one of cold weather, blackout, privation and preparation. Just before Christmas, the family ration books arrived in the post ready for rationing to start on Monday 8 January, 1940. It was to continue for fourteen years, finally ending in 1954 when meat came 'off ration'. Even the Royal Family was limited to exactly the same rations as everyone else. Before long, rationing was extended beyond the basics to include, sweets, milk, jam, biscuits, tinned food, breakfast cereals and meat.

When they arrived, ration books had to be registered with specific grocers so that supplies could be ordered in advance. Mum registered some of ours at Wrensons and some at the Co-op where she could save a 'dividend' and some at Mason's.

The books contained coupons which were used with money to buy a fixed amount of rationed food each week. We shopped every day. There were no fridges in most homes. Although we didn't have a fridge we did have a larder with a lovely cold slab to store food.

And so we queued every day, long, long, queues at every shop.

'Can we go to Masons?'

We loved the big store that had wires running in every direction under the ceiling. It was an 'overhead cash system.' People paid with cash. There were no bank cards, money was saved in the Post Office and withdrawn as needed. The money from a customer, plus the bill was put into a metal cup, which was then screwed into a container on the wire. At the pull of a lever, the cup was catapulted along wires to a cashier, hidden out of sight upstairs.

The bigger the store, the more wires. I watched as the cups whizzed round and then back again to exactly the right place, and then 'pinged' into the receiving nets. The change and the receipt were then removed and given to the customer.

'Which one is ours?' We competed with each other to guess, and watched for a cup to be launched. Excitement mounted as several traversed the wires at the same time.

The Grocer's shop had a smell of smoked bacon and cheeses. The Grocer wore a long white apron or a white coat and knew all his customers by name. Individual rations varied during wartime and so he took differing amounts of butter from a large slab and then patted it into smaller blocks with wooden paddles. Sugar was also weighed individually into blue paper bags—the price of sugar was fixed at the 1939 price of 3d per lb. for the duration of the war. Tea, which was sold as loose tea leaves, wasn't put on ration until July 1941 when the allowance was two ounces per person per week. That would have been a huge blow to my mother and father. A cup of tea was the first response to any problem.

In spite of rationing we still had treats. On Friday night, Dad gave Mary and me a penny each and we ran the few yards to Mrs Waggett's corner shop in Church Street. He stood at the door and watched until we came back safely. It was an old fashioned corner shop that sold all sorts of everything, but best of all were the sweets in big glass bottles. Tier upon tier of shelves, with bottles of brightly coloured sweets lined one wall. So many bottles, so many different colours and so many shapes of sweets.

'Which do you want dear?' asked Mrs Waggett.

'Dolly mixtures please.'

The sweets clattered into the brass weighing scales. Pink, lavender, black juicy jellies, yellow coconut squares. I watched as the weight tipped the scales—always hoping for just one more tiny sweet. Mrs Waggett smiled, as she tipped the multi-coloured sweets into a conical paper bag and twisted over the top. Sometimes we paid for our 'pennorth' of sweets with four farthings, which equalled one penny. Mrs Waggett, lovely name, always meant sweets to me over the years.

A farthing was a term meaning a fourth part of a penny and was English currency, from the thirteenth century until 1960. There were 4 farthings to a penny and 12 old pennies to a shilling.

Across the nation, British Restaurants were opened in city centres to serve cheap but nutritious meals which didn't require coupons. Many women were working, so workers ate at factory canteens, or British Restaurants. Lyons tea shops and Corner Houses were popular and food was reasonably priced.

In anticipation of war, millions of tons of food had already been imported. However, it was obvious that Britain would need to be self-supporting. Ships with food would be an obvious target for German bombs. People were encouraged to grow as much food as possible and Birmingham Council announced that seven thousand allotments had been made available—in addition to the fourteen thousand already in existence. Parks, playing fields, railway embankments and road verges were dug up and 'Dig for Victory' was a well-known slogan seen on posters.

There were fines for wasting food and smelly, communal 'pig swill' bins on every street. Vegetable peelings and any inevitable food waste, was collected by the City Council and used to feed the pigs which were an essential part of the British wartime diet. Hens and rabbits were bred for food in many back gardens across the country.

Children were allowed free cod liver oil, milk and orange juice to make sure they got enough vitamins and calcium. I loved the rose hip syrup or raspberry vinegar we had every day. There was also a lovely, sweet malt extract we had on a spoon. All children had a free bottle of milk in school as the government ensured every child got essential nutrients.

Petrol was rationed immediately war started in September, but not so many people had cars in those days. Wherever possible, horse-drawn vehicles were used for delivering goods to save petrol for the war effort. Coal, milk and bread came by horse and cart and the road was often referred to as the 'horse road.'

Someone else who came by horse and cart was the Rag and Bone man. He could be heard from a distance shouting 'Rags and bones', sometimes, 'Any old iron' and rolling the words into a long indecipherable sound that sounded almost musical. I always wondered why they wanted old bones, until I discovered they were used to make glue. Rags, bones, waste paper and metals, were all collected for salvage for planes, guns, ships and ammunition. Even railings outside schools and churches were removed and salvaged.

SAVING BRITAIN

But rusty old saucepans and iron railings would not pay for the war we were embarking on and Britain was still in debt to the USA from the first world war.

So how was money to be raised? Money to pay for hurricanes and spitfires, warships and submarines, for machine guns and ammunition. For building new factories and the money to pay men and women to work in them. As well as the money to support vast numbers of soldiers, sailors and airmen to fight for us. And at the end of the war, the money to rebuild blitzed and broken cities and reclaim bombsites from weeds and barbed wire. How was the money to be raised?

Something amazing happened. People on the home front entered into the war as determinedly as those on the battle field. Every section of society responded and British people made massive contributions to the cost of the war *out of their own pockets through the War Savings Campaign.*

Some people called it the 'blitz spirit' others said it was because it was 'the people's war'— a WW2 slogan. After the salvage of railings and saucepans, after increases in income tax and fresh debts to the USA and Canada, money was raised from the working man's pocket. Not begrudgingly but willingly, every man gave as much as he could.

The Government issued savings stamps which were stuck onto cards, these were exchanged when full for savings certificates. There were war bonds, premium bonds and victory bonds. They were to fund wartime expenditure and would be repaid after the war at 2% interest.

More than 6,000 school savings groups started in 1940 and many schools started 'Spitfire Funds.' There were street savings groups and small office groups and bigger savings groups from village to large cities. Each community was set a monetary target to support an airman, sailor or soldier or to buy a spitfire or a warship, or ammunition and machine guns. Prices were issued — £20,000 for a Wellington Bomber ... £40,000 for a Lancaster ... £138 for a bomb etc.

All this from people already highly taxed and short of money and working long hours in the war effort. Morale was raised and everyone was united and determined to win the 'People's War'.

'£ the enemy for all you are worth,' was a clever slogan seen on posters. Communities held carnivals and festivals, bands played, flags flew, men marched to promote the savings campaigns, and one town parade had 6 elephants to encourage people to turn out and to dip into their pockets. Thousands turned out to cheer. Local newspapers supported and reported events which were organised. Each village and town competed with others to save the most.

Perhaps one of the greatest attractions was in 1943, when Sir Robert Kindersley introduced Wings for Victory week in Trafalgar Square: *These weeks are the nation's salute to the gallant men of the Royal Air Force, of the Fleet Air Arm, and of the Allied Air Force... I shall release thirteen hundred pigeons each bearing a message to one of our savings committees throughout the country'.*

My mother wrote to her friend, 'The girls' school had a big effort for 'Wings for Victory' savings week. Every day they had to take savings and Bill finished the week for them and bought them each a certificate. They had nine 15s certificates between them.' I remember we bought 6d stamps with images of Princess Elizabeth and Margaret on them and stuck them onto cards. Of course it was Mum and Dad who were making the saving. She continued, *'Birmingham collected 16 million pounds for 'Wings for Victory' during that week.'* That was a huge amount for war wearied people to collect in one week.

And so the money for war was raised. Saved by the single 6d stamp at individual level; and by communities coming together for large-scale campaigns in different years such as the Spitfire Fund ... War Weapons Week ... Warship Weeks ... Wings for Victory and Salute the Soldier Week.

By the end of 1945, the amazing figure of nearly £2 billion had been saved by British people. But at the end of the war Britain still had an immense debt of £21 billion. The last US loan was not paid off until 2006.

4

SHATTERED DREAMS

And so Annie and Bill found themselves waiting for war for a second time in their lives. They had been in Birmingham just three years and loved their adopted hometown. Bill quickly found employment as an electrical and mechanical engineer, with a fancy goods and stationary manufacturer. They thought things were looking up at last.

As a first step, they rented a Victorian terraced house in Church Street Lozells. It was built in the 1890s and about 45 years old. The houses were good quality and modern for the time. They are now in the Lozells conservation area. Number seven had electric lighting—the old fashioned sort with brown Bakelite two pin plugs and switches—and hot and cold water. Each house had a tiny front garden but those have gone today in order to widen the narrow pavement. Between the houses, a side entry accessed a long back garden. The end of the garden backed onto an open space belonging to the local Primary School which was used as a playground.

A year after they moved to Birmingham I was born in Heathfield Maternity Hospital. It was just around the corner from Church Street. According to practice my Mother spent the next ten days 'lying in.' It was May 1937, the time of apple blossom and bluebells, blue skies and fresh green leaves. I was christened six weeks later at Villa Cross Methodist Church, a few minutes' walk from home and my name was inscribed on the decorated cradle roll. Annie and Bill were thrilled to be extending their family.

Lozells Road was busy, with excellent shops and a good bus and tram service into the city. Annie enjoyed being at the centre of activity. After living in a country village and driving a pony and trap to market, city transport was exciting. She loved the big city stores and especially the Bull Ring. An added bonus was that Bill's sister, Kathleen and husband Eddie, lived three minutes away in Anglesey Street.

Today, Lozells is a very disadvantaged area; but in those days it was a community of close-knit families who had lived for several generations in the same area. It was a happy, friendly place. Many worked in the Jewellery Quarter, a few minutes' walk away. The householder, who previously lived at our house, was a gold and silver refiner, two doors away lived a 'lapidarist' or a precious stone setter.

Annie was a prolific letter writer and in recent years, some of her letters were given to me by cousins in England and Australia. They reflect life in times of war and peace.

In a letter to Australia in December 1938, Annie wrote, *'Life has taken a turn for the better, Bill enjoys his new work, it is varied and interesting and his pay is good,'* she continued, *'after lots of struggles and trials we have a comfortable home and have made a number of friends. I wish we had come years ago. I like Birmingham very much.'*

She wrote that letter just before a picture postcard 'White Christmas.' Biting east winds and blizzards, from early December 1938, brought the most widespread Christmas snow of the last century. Day after day, the snow fell deep and heavy across the country settling to over a foot and drifting in places to seventeen. Postmen struggled through blocked roads to deliver Christmas parcels and mail. Lakes and canals froze solid and excited skaters were enticed onto the ice for the first time for years. Christmas morning was crisp, clear and white. Newspaper headlines reported it as 'spectacular.'

There had been a sudden and unexpected onset of cold weather, and on 17 December, temperatures plunged from 41F to 21F in twelve hours—11 degrees of frost. The London Gas Light and Coke Company reported it had supplied more gas, during twenty-four hours, than at any previous time *since gas had been used in London from 1812.* It was cold!

That Christmas, a third baby had arrived, Ann was born in July. Disposable nappies were still a distant dream; the soft white squares, hanging on the line, froze in the wintry air. Beside them, Bill's long johns looked like stiff white legs. Annie laughed, she was happy. After many losses, she had a family around her, Bill was working; there was money to spare that white Christmas before war was declared.

For the first time, four-year-old Mary knew what to expect. 'I want a baby doll of my own,' she kept saying when Ann was born.

'You shall have one for Christmas,' promised Annie.

Mary's brown eyes sparkled with excitement as she helped to put up the decorations. The baby doll was waiting on Christmas morning, snugly tucked into a crib draped in pretty blue muslin. It was a good Christmas. There was money for presents, a turkey to roast, Dad's sister lived close by and snow was falling. Bing Crosby sang, 'Too marvellous for words' and 'The way you look tonight.' Songs we were still singing decades later.

It was Christmas 1938; nine months later war was declared.

Although happy in Church Street, it was only temporary. Annie and Bill had plans to buy a house further out of town. After moving to Birmingham, they started to save with the Ideal Benefit Society. In the days before National Insurance, this Friendly Society provided social security for Birmingham working people. It combined sick benefit, pensions, maternity benefit and a savings bank.

The Society had also diversified and was building a model housing estate for those who saved with their bank. Cherry Orchard Estate was commenced in 1935 on farmland and cherry orchards, right on the edge of the countryside. It was to have wide roads, shops, landscaped open places, a school and houses of varying designs. The aim was 'houses for health.' Annie and Bill, along with Bill's sister Kath, were each saving for a house on the estate. The cost was £425, or a deposit and 11s a week mortgage repayments.

At the brick laying ceremony, the Lord Mayor of Birmingham said the Society was, 'Providing houses under the happiest of conditions, on the borders of the country and yet within easy reach of the city.'

The smart, semi-detached houses were attractive and a new style in the 1930s. The exciting designs reflected the aspirations of many young couples during the more prosperous years of the 1930s. A very new design in the 1930s, but today, just one of countless others countrywide. Modern luxuries included fashionable electric fires in the bedrooms, tiled bathrooms and a very modern kitchen for the time. Buyers were able to choose colour schemes, tiles, fireplaces and some of the kitchen fitments.

These houses represented a new way of life in a world recovering from the first world war and determined to move on from austerity and hardship. Bill's sister had already moved into one of the houses. The bay windows flooded the house with light, it had a large garden and was in a pleasant road. Next it was Bill and Annie's turn.

What fun it must have been as the two couples excitedly made plans and dreamt of how they would furnish their new homes.

There are few photographic records of those days but I have a small, tattered Brownie photo, of our family in the garden of Kath's house with 'Lloyd Road' written on the back. Ann looks about a year old, so it is 1939. Lupins are in full bloom so it is May or June and we are sitting in deckchairs. The sun is at its height and the shadows are short and as I know where the sun sets, it is just before lunch. Dad is with us and because he worked a 48-hour week, including Saturday morning, it must be Sunday.

So much from one photo. A hot summer Sunday in 1939 when, oblivious to what was to happen, Annie and Bill would surely have been discussing their plans to move.

Three months later they had finally saved the deposit for their dream house and went to the Society Office to start negotiations; it was the very same weekend that war was announced. They were too late.

'I'm sorry we can't build any more houses at the present.'

'But why? . . . we have the deposit and were hoping to move quickly because of the war.'

'I am sorry but we have just been told today by the Government, to stop further building.'

Annie was so upset. 'Is there no chance at all? ... Bill's sister has just moved there, we so hoped.'

The Officer had been turning many away. 'We have half-built houses but we can't finish them or build more. The Government is diverting all building materials and man-power for the war effort.'

Bill and Annie learned that in a special meeting, Birmingham Corporation had ordered immediate suspension of all new building. Their short experience of a better future collapsed. Now, when they thought they were settled into a better life, it was to be war again.

Like many others nationwide, they were never again in the position to buy their own house. After the war, their deposit had gone and there was a shortage of building materials. Prices soared. Before the war, a private house in Cherry Orchard cost around £400; after the war, the cost of building a semi-detached *council house* is recorded at £1600. This was Birmingham, the most bombed city after London, and houses both to rent and to buy were in short supply.

And so we stayed in Church Street.

By the Spring of 1940 the news from Europe was ominous. The battle was getting close to home. Would we be invaded? Hitler said he would take Britain — the last country standing against him.

The Home Guard was formed in May 1940. The Government made an urgent appeal on the radio to all men aged between 17 and 65. They wanted men, not already serving in the armed forces, to become part-time soldiers. Within 24 hours of the radio broadcast, a quarter of a million had volunteered. By the end of July this number had risen to over a million. Many who joined the Home Guard, could not join the regular army because their day time jobs were necessary to keep the country running. They included farm workers, bakers, teachers, grocers, bank staff and railway workers. Other men were either too young or too old to join the army.

The men were given *military style training* and, at first, they had no uniforms and little equipment. The public were invited to give their shotguns and pistols to the Home Guard and within a few months over 20 thousand weapons were handed in. They really *were* called Dad's Army.

5

DUNKIRK

For the previous six months, war had developed on different fronts on the continent. Germany invaded Poland, Denmark and Norway; then in May 1940, invaded Holland, Belgium and then Luxembourg. And now Hitler vowed to invade Britain, the last country standing against him.

On Friday 10 May, Neville Chamberlain resigned and Winston Churchill became Prime Minister. Churchill believed it was his destiny to lead the country in war. He took over just in time to oversee the evacuation of Dunkirk. He made a memorable speech to the country on 13 May. It was a speech that inspired and invigorated the British people to fight as never before.

> *'I have nothing to offer but blood, toil, tears, and sweat. We have before us an ordeal of the most grievous kind. We have before us many, many months of struggle and suffering. You ask, what is our policy? I say it is to wage war by land, sea, and air. War with all our might and with all the strength God has given us, and to wage war against a monstrous tyranny never surpassed in the dark and lamentable catalogue of human crime.'*

A British Expeditionary Force was sent to France at the start of the war to help patrol a two-hundred-mile length of the French and Belgian frontier. It was a powerful fighting unit but after the surrender of the Belgian army and against a massive German onslaught; they were forced back from the frontiers and then onto the beaches at Dunkirk.

In May 1940, thousands of British, French and Canadian troops were cut off by the German army and stranded on the beaches. They were unprotected targets against the Luftwaffe who were merciless in their bombing of the soldiers on the beaches.

The King called for a National Day of Prayer, many attended services throughout the land. The Archbishop of Canterbury led prayers 'for our soldiers in dire peril in France'. The country began to realise the desperate plight of the troops and prayed for a miraculous delivery.

In the tunnels under Dover castle, a plan was formed to bring the soldiers back from the beaches of Dunkirk. It was code-named 'Operation Dynamo.' Ships of every size and condition were requisitioned, and calls went out for volunteers with private boats and vessels of any kind. In less than a week, a total of 693 ships were drawn together and included, 39 Destroyers and 36 Minesweepers, the rest was made up of trawlers, passenger ferries and a flotilla of fishing boats, pleasure craft and lifeboats. The men who sailed from the ports that lined the English Channel, were from every walk of life and often amateurs.

In the evacuation more than 338 thousand Allied soldiers were rescued from the beaches and the harbour of Dunkirk. Many troops were ferried onto British destroyers. Others had to wade from the beaches toward the ships, waiting for hours shoulder deep in the water. Thousands were rescued by what became known as the 'Little ships of Dunkirk' which made repeated journeys back and forth across the Channel. The Medway Queen, a paddle steamer, rescued seven thousand men in seven trips.

For the ten days of the evacuation, the Luftwaffe bombed the soldiers on the beaches as well as the ships rescuing them. There was nowhere to hide. Bodies lay on the beaches and in the water. The sand was red with blood and wounded men lay everywhere. The flames from Dunkirk could be seen from the sea as the rescue craft crossed the channel. The evacuation was completed on 4 June, 1940.

The Daily Express on 31 May, 1940, wrote about 'History's Strangest Armada,' as tens of thousands came home by day and night. . .The following is an excerpt:

'Under the guns of the British Fleet and the wings of the Air Force a large proportion of the Expeditionary Force have now returned. The Army is coming back from Belgium. It is a dirty, tired, hungry army that has been shelled and bombed from three sides.

There was a touch of glory about these men, tramping along a pier, still in formation, still with their rifles, still with a grin on their oily bearded faces. They were exhausted, had not slept or eaten for days, many tramped in stockinged feet and shirt sleeves. Many had wounds and torn uniforms. They saluted their Officers who stood in ragged mackintoshes and said, 'Thank you Sir.'

How can I tell you of these men. . .It is the greatest and most glorious sight I have ever seen. They came ashore in heaps, scarcely able to stand, yet they pulled themselves into straight lines. . . one with a head wound, another with a torn trouser leg soaked in blood, another with his arm tied up with a scarf. Many soldiers arrived with only a vest and socks. It was pitiful.

They were met by people living near the harbour, who went to see what was happening, they went back, raided their pantries, gathered sheets and blankets from beds, and went to help. All day and all night they handed out cups of tea, cigarettes and lumps of bread.

The men cheered to the crowds, 'Don't worry, we'll get them yet.' One young French lad staggered out of the ship and said, 'England God bless it.' Hilde Marchant.

Winston Churchill described the evacuation of Dunkirk, as a 'miracle of deliverance' but also said it was the greatest military defeat for many centuries, saying the whole root, core and brain of the British Army was stranded in Dunkirk.

The RAF lost 474 planes and six British and three French destroyers were sunk, along with nine large rescue boats. Although so many did come home, many did not and the dreaded telegram began arriving in British homes. This was the quickest way of informing families that a loved one was missing in action or killed. Thousands received those telegrams. The telegram was followed up by a letter personally signed by King George.

In June, France surrendered after the retreat of the Allied Forces from Dunkirk. *Britain was alone.* Immediately after the evacuation the French Brigadier, Charles de Gaulle, arrived in England to organise a French Resistance. He asked if he could use the BBC to convey messages to the French people encouraging them to resist the occupation. Every evening at 8 pm, he went on air and encouraged the French to resist. The stories of the resistance, the courage and the heroism became part of the folk history of both Britain and France.

But Britain was indeed alone. Churchill made another famous speech on 4 June 1940.

'We shall go on to the end, we shall fight in France, we shall fight on the seas and oceans, we shall fight with growing confidence and growing strength in the air, we shall defend our Island, whatever the cost may be, we shall fight on the beaches, we shall fight on the landing grounds, we shall fight in the fields and in the streets, we shall fight in the hills; we shall never surrender.'

6

AT HOME IN CHURCH STREET

At home in church Street Mum and Dad listened to the radio and read the papers and heard what Winston Churchill said—*We shall defend our Island, whatever the cost, we shall fight on the beaches, we shall fight on the landing grounds, we shall fight in the fields and in the streets, we shall fight in the hills; we shall never surrender.*

Would it really come to this? We children knew nothing about the threatening terror from the skies. I didn't know it was the phoney war and I didn't realise all adult eyes were on the retreat from Dunkirk and were scouring papers and listening to the radio for what would happen next. Mum and Dad made life as normal as possible. There would be three months before the bombs started dropping.

My awakening memories are of life from a child's perspective. To me number seven was just a happy home. I can walk through the house in my 'mind's eye.' It was a typical small Victorian terrace house, well built and modern for its time. The front door opened into a hall with a sitting room on the right. Some things stand out in my 'mind-walk'. . .the small organ which Dad taught himself to play. . .the treadle sewing machine which Mum used to make clothes and brightly coloured rugs. . .the sash window overlooking a tiny garden. . .the door to the cellar by the fireplace.

I really didn't like the door to the cellar. I wondered what was down those winding stairs. I ran away whenever the door was opened. So what *was* down there? A mound of black shiny coal. Mum complained that the coal delivered by the coal-man was 'all slack,' no lumps, just little nuggets that wouldn't burn. Coal was rationed.

When the coal man came Mary shouted 'Come and see.' We watched as he opened the grate over the coal-shute below the window. The man's face and hands were covered with black dust and he carried a huge sack of coal on his back. He heaved it up and tipped it down that shute and we watched him through the window. His eyes glinted through the grime on his face and so did his teeth when he smiled at us watching him. We giggled as we watched the horse and cart, loaded with sacks of coal, clip-clop down the road.

Along the hall, was the back room where Mum cooked on a gas cooker. There was a grate which needed 'black-leading' and often some brightly coloured spills on the mantle-piece to light the fire. Attached to the back room was a scullery, in there was a huge giant of a mangle which towered over me. Every Monday it was hauled into place. It was always Monday washing, Tuesday ironing, Wednesday cleaning, Thursday shopping, Friday baking and so it went in houses across the country. Wash-day lasted all day and started early.

On Monday morning, Mum was up whilst still dark to fill the boiler and heat water for the washing. When ready, white clothes and sheets were added and boiled first and then the water and washing was transferred to the big dolly tub and 'dollied. A dolly had a long wooden handle, with five wooden pegs at the bottom for agitating the clothes in soapy water.

It seems like a human washing machine to me now. Round and back swirling the clothes, round and back, again and again went the dolly in Mum's strong hands until the washing was thoroughly clean. Mum used Sunlight hard soap, Rinso powder and also Reckitt's blue to whiten the whites. After the whites, coloured clothes were washed in the dolly tub. Sometimes she used Lux soap flakes in Birmingham's soft water and the swirling of the dolly made mounds of white suds.

We watched and waited and then, 'Here you are,' she filled a bowl from the tub. This was what we were waiting for.

'Where are the pipes?' The soapy water was perfect for blowing bubbles.

'Wait a minute.' She took the pipes from a drawer. They looked like old-fashioned white smoking pipes used by Victorian gentlemen, and then she put the bowl of soap on the garden path.

We dipped the white pipes into the water and blew. Clusters of rainbow bubbles drifted off and away as we watched and tried to catch them—but they just burst and popped. We chased and squealed and laughed.

Mum got on with the washing. She lifted the clean clothes onto the rollers on the mangle. Then the handle was turned taking the clothes through and water was squeezed out and back into the dolly tub. I loved watching the steaming water cascading from the sheets as they went through the rollers and then came out on the other side almost dry and flattened. It felt very satisfying. The process was repeated several times through a rinsing cycle.

In summer, clothes were dried on a line in the garden supported by a clothes prop; they came inside smelling of fresh air. In winter, they were dried on a big wooden clothes horse in front of the fire. I hated those days. The room was dark except for the firelight, and it was impossible to get near the fire because of steaming washing. It always had to be dried before Dad got home. It took a whole day to wash, rinse, starch and then dry the clothes ready for ironing.

Ironing was another task that seemed to take hours and Mum never cut corners. She ironed everything. I don't think she expected wash-day to ever be any different. It was many years before she was proud to own a washing machine. There was no time to cook on wash-days so dinner was usually the cold meat, leftover from the Sunday joint, with chips. Sometimes we had bubble 'n squeak which was made from leftover potatoes and cabbage, fried together and topped with brown sauce and we loved that.

The stairs to the bedrooms went off the hall and had a narrow strip of carpet, fastened on each step with four-inch stair-rods. Why is heavy rain described as coming down in 'stair-rods'? The banister and the woodwork were stained dark brown.

There were three bedrooms and Mary and I shared a big double bed in a room overlooking the back garden. The bed was high and difficult to climb onto and had an old fashioned mesh base that bounced and bounced. As Mum tucked us in, she told stories of her childhood or sang the popular songs of those days. Sometimes she recited a poem which she had learned as a child, 'I remember, I remember the house where I was born.'

'Say it again', we begged. . .anything to keep her talking. 'And tell us about Spout Hollow.' We always wanted to know about the cottage where she and Dad lived when they were first married. She told us that the cottage was very small and in the bedrooms they had to kneel to look out of the window. Sometimes Mum talked about Peter and Cathleen, their children who had died in the cottage—she cried, and we all cried with her.

'Why was it called Spout Hollow?' We already knew the answer but wanted to stop her going downstairs.

'Because there was a water spout in the bank in the lane; I had to collect all the water I used from the spout.' We were fascinated, water came from a tap, not a spout in a bank.

'Now tell us about your grandmother—Grannie Annie.' We heard the stories so often but we still wanted to hear them again.

'She lived in Spout Hollow as well', she said, 'and she kept chickens and knew how to make money—she always had money in her big pockets for the grandchildren.'

'What about Grandad, why doesn't he come here.' And so she told us again about the family she missed so much. How her father went ahead of the family to Australia to find a place to live. How he stood on the doorstep and said 'I'll see you all next year.'

Mum said a year later a telegram came saying, 'Come and join me.' He had bought a fruit farm. Annie was torn between the vision of a pioneer life in Australia and marrying Bill. Love won and she stayed behind to marry.

'I never saw my Mum or Dad again.' She always cried and said that one day we would join the family in Australia.

Eventually she told us to settle down. When she'd gone, we jumped up to bounce on the bed; higher and higher we jumped, it was like a trampoline. After that we ran around in circles chanting 'round and round the garden', until we fell down dizzy. When we got tired, we played make believe games, imagining the 'fairy land' hidden under the covers that we had just trampled into mounds. Lying flat on our stomachs we tried to spy around the corners into the tunnels made by the folds. Robert Louis Stevensen wrote a child's poem, about a similar make believe land, called 'The Land of the Counterpane.'

We finally went to sleep, and then Mum came upstairs to straighten the tangled sheets.

On Sundays we went to Aston Villa Methodist Church where Dad was the Choir Master. He took me to a choir rehearsal one evening; I was so proud to be with him and remember how small I felt and how tall everyone seemed. There were legs everywhere. I clung to his trousers until he picked me up and showed me the Cradle Roll on the wall.

'That is your name', he said pointing to Muriel Angela and the date in beautiful copper plate writing. 'That's when you were christened here.'

And so the year of the phoney war dragged on. Every evening, barrage balloons tethered by steel cables and filled with a light gas, were raised around the city, just in case raids started that night. Every morning they were lowered. . .What next after the evacuation of Dunkirk? Would there be an invasion?

During the prolonged evacuation from Dunkirk, the RAF lost 474 planes the German Air Force also lost many aircraft and crews. There was a temporary lull as both sides replaced their losses. By the beginning of July 1940, the Luftwaffe had built up to 2600 bombers and fighters. The RAF built up strength to 640 Hurricane and Spitfire fighter planes. A great disparity in numbers.

Hitler had said he would invade Britain, the last country standing against him. His first aim was to destroy the RAF either in the air or on the ground in South East England.

The Battle for Britain began in July but intensified on 13 August, on 'Eagle Day' as it was called by the German High Command. Wave after wave of German bombers attacked the coastal targets and airfields. Valiant young British airmen, in Spitfires and Hurricanes dived, swooped, evaded and targeted the enemy planes. The RAF had the advantage of being over home ground. Planes could be quickly refuelled and put back into the air. German aircraft, however, were lost if they came down.

The battle raged and on 20 August, Winston Churchill made the speech that will always be identified with the Battle of Britain.

'Never in the field of human conflict has so much been owed by so many to so few.'

That summer became known as the 'Spitfire Summer'. Other aircraft were involved but it was the 'Spitfire', and their dashing young pilots that most people remember. Hitler said he would be in Britain by 15 August. He was not in Britain by 15 August. He did not gain the victory he expected over the RAF in the skies over South East England and switched his tactics to bombing raids on British cities.

7

THE BIRMINGHAM BLITZ

On 4 June 1940 Churchill said. '*We shall go on to the end. . .we shall never surrender.*' Britain did not surrender but was tested to the uttermost.

In August the 'Blitz' by the Luftwaffe began over Britain. Blitz comes from the German word 'blitzkrieg', meaning lightning war.

More than 5,100 High Explosive bombs and thousands more incendiary bombs, would be dropped on Birmingham in seventy-seven raids, during the next eight months. ARP records indicate the first bombs were dropped one month *before* the first blitz on London. The City was prepared, but the year of the phoney war had dulled the edge of readiness.

Annie and Bill, wearied by a year of austerity, the anxiety of Dunkirk and the Battle for Britain, went to bed on 9 August 1940, not realising this would be the first of many nights of terror. They awakened suddenly at 1am, to the sound of bombs dropping and explosions. Shocked out of sleep and bewildered, they rushed to get the family into the shelter. There had been no siren warnings.

RAF and ARP records of the time, indicate that the raids were sporadic during early August, however, from the twenty-fourth there were five consecutive nights of intense raids with several hundred tons of High Explosive bombs dropped on the City Centre. One of the early casualties of war, was the much loved Market Hall in the Bull Ring, which was flattened and ablaze on the night of 25 August. By morning the roof had gone and it was left a charred ruin of iron beams, twisted metal and rubble within blackened walls.

On 9 September 1940, Annie wrote a hasty twelve-page letter to a friend describing what had been happening during the previous weeks—the following is an excerpt:

My dear H,

I have left everything to write you this letter. I have been trying to get the opportunity this last fortnight. There hasn't been time as we have been in the shelter every night for the last fifteen nights. We have not been to bed for three weeks. The last time we did go, we were awakened at one in the morning by bombs dropping and terrific gunfire. We had no warning, so you can guess we did not dare to go to bed afterwards.

The men around here got together and watched in turns for the Germans and then gave the alarm. That was three weeks ago. We have had proper warning for the last fortnight at times varying from half past eight to ten o' clock; so as soon as we have had tea we have to get ready. The raids have lasted until half past four at times. We put beds for the children in the front room downstairs so that they can go there until it is time to take them into the shelter.

There has been a lot of damage all around us. We have missed it so far. The nearest damage is at Six Ways, down Lozells Road. Eight houses were demolished there and several people were killed including two babies. Seven soldiers were killed trying to remove a time bomb. There were huge fires in town. C and A Modes was hit one night and several other big shops. We saw the blaze for hours. The Market Hall in town was brought down, just four stark walls left and it was a big place. The watchman let out the animals and birds. This place had a curious old time piece. Walsall Road was hit too and also Perry Barr. We have picked up lots of shrapnel in the garden and dozens of incendiary bombs have been dropped.

We feel very safe in the shelter although we can feel it vibrate at times when the heavy gun firing is on. Bill has made it very comfortable and we can lie down and get a little rest. At first I feel faint when the raids start but it soon passes. It would be luxury to go to bed and stay for eight hours without worrying about Germans and sirens. Still we are very optimistic and on the whole very cheerful. Nothing matters as long as we are spared. We and England can build again. Everything is possible if we try hard enough.

She did not realise this was only the beginning of another eight months of equally devastating raids. Perhaps she had taken courage from the Birmingham Mail headline of 6 September, which read: 'Not daunted; Birmingham's fine morale standing up to raids. Work goes on as usual.' My mother said we are 'optimistic and very cheerful,' she had no reason to pretend to her closest friend. In fact, her response to the many tragedies of her, life was to make the best of every situation. She never talked about the raids after the war; she was warm and not afraid of showing her feelings, so I don't know if she just buried those traumas.

In later years my mother talked about the curious old time piece in the Bull Ring which she mentions in her letter. She said it was a lovely old clock, with four carved mediaeval figures which moved to strike bells every quarter of an hour. The figures were painted in bright colours and the clock face was in gold leaf. Crowds gathered to see the bells strike. Dad thought it was amazing. I remember standing with him waiting for the figures to move out; that must have been during the summer of 1940 before the raids started.

Mum loved the old Bull Ring which was a hive of activity. Stall vendors shouted their wares, people stood on soap boxes preaching or shouting politics. Bands played and the smell of fast food filled the air. The huge iconic Market Hall had more than 600 stalls which sold produce of every kind—fish and meat, clothing or fabrics; pets in cages, china and inventive 'must haves' for the housewife of the day. It was noisy and exciting and there was always a bargain to be had, or street entertainment to be watched.

The night after the Market Hall was gutted, came another night of devastation. The raid began a short time after midnight. In the city centre, fires were blazing, warehouses, factories and shops were alight and the roadway itself melted, with the liquid fire running along to set more buildings alight. Ninety fire crews were involved in fighting the blazes.

These were the nights when we slept in the shelter for fifteen nights in a row. Nights when the city was changing daily, was devastated and broken.

I have some clear memories of the blitz on Birmingham which started when I was three-and-a-half. I can't anchor many memories to dates but I can hear, even now, the wails of the siren getting higher and higher in warning, and later the 'all clear' signal. The two sounds were very different. I can hear the drone in the distance and then the roar of bombers getting steadily nearer, sometimes a whistle followed by a long silence before an explosion which shook the shelter.

I remember searchlights sweeping across the sky as they watched for approaching planes; the thunderous 'ack-ack' of anti-aircraft guns as they targeted the German planes from the ground. From time to time I dream about those searchlights and of formation after formation of planes criss-crossing and coming simultaneously from every direction. They are very low, the sky is lit up and I can see the markings on the planes. I feel I am being watched and in my dream I try to hide but the planes 'eyes' follow me. I start to feel anxious and then wake up.

One night is particularly clear in my memory. At some point we had returned to sleeping in our beds upstairs. In the early hours of the morning. I woke suddenly. The sirens were wailing, the shrillness piercing the silence. It was pitch black indoors, the blackout curtains shut out every trace of light. In the house no-one was stirring. I waited for sounds.

'Mummy the sirens are going'. I knew we had to quickly get into the shelter. 'Mummy, Daddy get up.'

In that inky blackness I got out of bed and put on my little red dressing gown and slippers. It had become a nightly routine but on this night, no one else had woken. I felt my way to their room.

I remember standing by the top of their bed in the darkness saying, 'Get up, get up the sirens are going, wake up.'

Suddenly there was activity. They jumped out of bed, jolted awake.

'Quick, get Ann, Mary wake up.'

We were speedily whisked into the shelter. I felt pleased when Dad said, 'What a good girl you are.'

I was excited at sleeping in the shelter. It was cosy with the paraffin lamp casting shadows on the corrugated roof and blankets tucked firmly in place. Mum, and sometimes Dad, was with us and for an innocent child, it was a family adventure. We had drinks and food and stories until we dropped asleep.

I can't remember feeling afraid until I saw the biggest, blackest, longest legged, furry spider I have ever seen. An enormous denizen of the underground; we were in its territory. I can still see it now darting across the roof. I screamed; I was more afraid of a spider than a bomb. Mary was older and remembers the fear and tension as the bombs dropped.

The pressure stepped up. In October, there were raids and wailing sirens every single night for three out of four weeks. There was serious damage across the city. Fires raged every night and there were many fatalities. On the 26 October, a bomb exploded on a basement shelter in Barker Street three hundred yards from our home. Two members of the Aston home guard risked their lives helping people who were trapped. Kneeling in water, that was flooding the basement, with bare hands they removed loose beams supporting huge concrete blocks. Bombs continued to fall around but they fearlessly continued for three hours until all victims and dead were removed.

The Times Newspaper recorded their bravery when they were awarded the George medal in September 1942 'In recognition of conspicuous gallantry in carrying out hazardous work in a very brave manner.'

Heavy prolonged raids over those weeks in October damaged many gas and water mains and the centre of the city was repeatedly bombed. The railway station, the Council House, Town Hall, Cathedral and the Art gallery were hit. One cinema had a direct hit one night; sadly, nineteen people died in their seats. The City was described as a funeral pyre.

There were raids almost every night through November and bombs damaged Lozells Road yet again, for five nights out of the first nine in the month. A lot of the time Mum was on her own with us children. Dad was either on shift as a fire warden or on lookout with the local men in the road.

One night in the shelter there was a whistle—then silence. Everyone froze. There was a flash of light and a thud as a bomb dropped at the end of our back garden. Someone said, 'That was close.' I remember the thud; Mary remembers the shelter shaking. No house was hit in Church Street whilst we were there, but maps indicate a lot of incendiary bombs were dropped behind the house and around the local roads. Incendiary bombs were dropped to light up an area so that targets could be identified. They caused explosions and more fire damage than the 'HE', high explosive bombs which could demolish rows of houses.

There was little in the local papers about these raids. News reporting about Birmingham raids was censored. It was feared that the enemy would find out what had been damaged and use the information for the next raid, or as ammunition for propaganda and taunting. Birmingham was a key target because of the factories that produced a large number of the planes and ammunition necessary for the war effort. Up to four hundred thousand City people were involved in production and their lives were in constant danger. For more than a hundred years, Birmingham had been known as the 'City of a Thousand Trades.'

There were a number of factories that the Luftwaffe wanted to destroy, including Vickers-Armstrong at Castle Bromwich, which produced 12 thousand Spitfire fighter planes during the war. Longbridge Austin car factory was also a target and had switched to producing munitions. They produced over eight million shells and thousands of planes. In addition, Birmingham Small Arms company, (BSA) comprising 67 factories, made arms and ammunition including over one million rifles, machine guns and motorcycles for the armed forces.

The Government needed to know how people were coping with the air-raids and the privations of war, so a group of volunteer observers were asked to record the feelings and experiences of the British public. Their reports were to be analysed by the government to test public morale during difficult times. Newspapers were not allowed to publish negative reports and were not a reliable source.

The volunteers were from the Mass-Observation group, which had been founded in 1937, to record everyday life of ordinary people in Britain by collecting stories and overheard comments. Volunteers were asked to record a day-to-day account of their lives during wartime in the form of a diary. The intention was to inform the government of the real feelings of the British public. Observations included conversations overheard in shelters on air raids, blackout, rationing, ARP and the wearing of gas masks. As no special instructions were given, diaries varied greatly. The surveys provided the basis of weekly intelligence reports for the Ministry of Information. Mass-Observation was criticised by some as an invasion of privacy. Participants were not only reporting on their own lives; they often commented on their neighbours and friends as well. Mass-Observation is today housed at the University of Sussex and used by students, academics, media researchers for its collection of material on everyday life in Britain.

There was one night that my mother often talked about with great sadness, the night of 14 November, 1940. That night, in 'Operation Moonlight Sonata', three quarters of Coventry factories and infrastructure as well as four thousand homes were totally destroyed. Coventry was a mediaeval city of great beauty, comparable to York and Bath, with half-timbered buildings and alleyways. The famous Cathedral was demolished apart from four stark walls and fire destroyed the beautiful city centre. Coventry was also an industrial city producing a range of products, engines and aero accessories. For fifteen hours, 450 German bombers dropped High Explosive bombs destroying water supplies, the electricity network and gas mains. Hundreds of incendiary bombs set the city on fire. The raid reached its climax around midnight, one volunteer from Mass Observation recalled, 'It was a satanic sight, fire raging all around us and everywhere chaos, rubble and destruction.'

Mum's closest childhood friend lived in Coventry and she knew the city well. Years later she talked about the beautiful city that had been destroyed.

Mass-Observation investigators, sent to assess the situation the next day, reported, 'There were open signs of hysteria, terror—the overwhelmingly dominant feeling was one of utter helplessness. . .the impact of the previous night had left people practically speechless.' The German High Command described the destruction of Coventry as a reprisal for a British raid on Munich, on 8 September, where Hitler was speaking at a rally. After this the Germans invented a new word and boasted they would 'coventrate' Birmingham next.

Five nights later they did just that.

Raids on Birmingham continued almost every night through November, but on the nineteenth, the raids entered a new dimension of ferocity when 350 German bombers blitzed Birmingham. They came in wave after wave for nine interminable hours and dropped thousands of bombs. Warehouses and factories blazed. One hundred gas mains were damaged, railways were hit and a large number of houses and shops were demolished.

Carl Chinn in 'Brum Undaunted' records: 'This horrific raid began on Tuesday 19 November, when the first of the 350 planes dropped flares and incendiaries, lighting up their targets for the heavy bombers to drop their slivers of death. Ten minutes later Fisher and Ludlow's factory was hit.'

'From 7pm, the tele-printer in Birmingham's Control Centre, sent messages, minute by minute to the Ministry of Home Security. Each minute gave news of another German hit–Raid, heavy and widespread– Fire position getting worse–Factory damage–New Street Station hit–Chance Brothers hit–Wilmot Breedon damage– Nine factories hit– BSA Small Heath – So the messages sped all night to London.'

The BSA Small Heath munitions factory received a direct hit. The factory blazed and concrete floors collapsed in the explosions, bringing heavy machinery down into the basement where workers were sheltering. Many were trapped and died in the basement. The rescue work went on all night. The Birmingham and Warwick canal was pumped dry by the Fire Brigade in their attempts to control the fire. A total of sixty fire crews attended the scene. Many medals were awarded for bravery in the rescue.

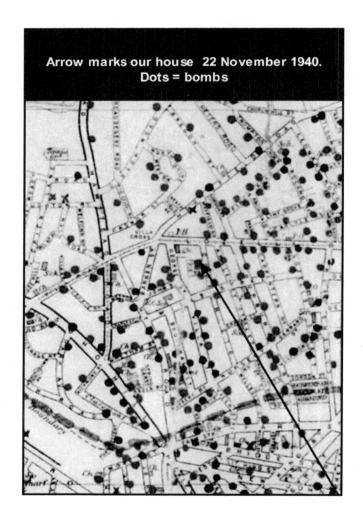

8

NOVEMBER 22 — FIRE STORMS

The worst raid was yet to come three nights later on 22 November. It was a night that would never be forgotten. Sirens went early at seven in the evening and the 'All clear' was not until 5:30am. Hundreds of German aircraft bombed the city in a relentless attack for ten hours. The city was traversed systematically from south-east to north-west and then north-east to south-west. 'It was a clear night and the planes dived low to aim at their targets. *Some people reported they could see the pilots looking* right *at them and firing machine guns I think this may be the night I dream about, when planes are 'chasing' me.*

It was a concentrated raid right across the City and particularly on the City Centre. The RAF records that 870 High Explosive bombs, landmines and thousands of incendiaries were dropped. As the huge HE bombs made impact, they exploded and flattened Civic Centre buildings as well as whole streets and blocks of houses. They made deep craters, fracturing gas mains and causing further gas explosions. Fire from incendiaries ripped through adjacent houses and buildings.

On that night, Bill was fire-watching and Annie was alone with us children when the siren went around seven in the evening. She just had time to get us into the shelter before the first bombs dropped. Remembering the previous terrifying raid, she shuddered at the steady roar of approaching planes. Anti-aircraft guns started to respond; the ground shook and the shelter vibrated as the guns thundered. It drove home the point that enemy planes were right overhead—they were firing at targets on the ground—they were firing at her family in the shelter.

During that night, several incendiary bombs fell on Washwood Heath Gasworks. The Times newspaper in 1942, described how the crown of one of the gas-holders was alight with a 'plume' of flame. The gas-holder was 200-foot-high and four men climbed to the top, carrying sacks and bags of bags of clay, which they dropped into the gas-holder. They extinguished the fire and stopped the escape of gas. *No protective equipment was carried and a raid was still in progress in the area.* The men must have been visible to planes overhead. They were awarded the George Medal for bravery.

The entire city was pummelled for hour after hour. Annie listened to the whistle and crash of dropping bombs, the explosions, the sound of breaking glass and falling masonry and the ringing of fire engine bells racing to fires. It was relentless and never ending. If only Bill was here. . .if only she had gone to Australia. Sleep was impossible. What if Bill didn't come back. . .what would she do if the house was hit. . .if the shelter was hit. . .what if?

She must have thought she wouldn't survive the night. Her mind went over the losses in her thirty-eight years, her sister who died when she was seventeen, her family of seven who emigrated to Australia leaving her behind, the grandmother she was so close to. She thought of her lovely mother who died in Australia and her first two babies. Tears came to her eyes as she thought of Cathleen and Peter. Now she had three treasures to protect. She felt so helpless.

Occasionally the street warden brought news, 'Sorry Annie, there's no news about Bill, it's terrible out there; the whole city is on fire, lots of factories and five cinemas have been hit, seven police stations have gone.'

We children slept fitfully. Six-year-old Mary kept waking nervously, 'What's that noise?' Annie quietened her. Eventually, sometime around midnight, she went out onto the path to look towards Bill's factory—it was blazing. I heard her move and joined her. I have a vivid memory of that night of six hundred fires.

'Dad is on fire watch in that factory' she said, pointing to flames that were leaping towards the sky. From horizon to horizon, the sky was glowing brilliant red and orange. I can see and remember the smell of smoke and the noise of explosions.

The all clear finally sounded at six in the morning, after eleven relentless hours. Annie stumbled out of the shelter. According to records there was no water in the city and no gas. . .she lit the fire to boil water from a bucket to make a cup of tea.

Bill finally came home, safe but exhausted. 'Annie, there are fires everywhere and there's no water to put them out.'

Mum and Dad were at the heart of this destruction. If there had been television, Mum would have seen the grim report of the night's carnage and destruction hour by hour.

The city was ablaze with six hundred fires; one thousand Fire Fighters worked to put them out as rescuers searched for survivors in the rubble, they dug at rubble with bare hands or with pick and shovel. And then the dangerous work of de-fusing one hundred unexploded bombs perched in precarious positions began. They were ticking time bombs ready to detonate and kill.

A secret Government Report, released in 1974, said the blitzed City was close to chaos and in danger of becoming uninhabitable. These facts were censored. The Government said in 1939 that Birmingham's importance to the war industry is essential; the Germans must not know if the Luftwaffe penetrates the City defences.

The City Water Department needed five days to repair the damage. *There was no water and the next night the City was defenceless.* Royal Engineers were called in ready to explode fire breaks if necessary. Harry Klopper writing in the 'Fight against Fire' said: 'If the enemy had struck again immediately, there is little doubt that Birmingham would have been practically destroyed by fire.'

Unbelievably, the RAF reported that after the three raids ending 22 November, the City was almost back to normal a week later. Water and gas mains had been repaired, only two electricity trunk cables remained to be repaired, transport services were reported to be practically normal and more than two thirds of the sewers repaired.

Churchill said '*We will not surrender.*'

Railways were also back to normal. Railways were national targets because of their essential role in the movement of food supplies, troops to camps and embarkation points and of ammunition for the war effort. The country could not have survived without them; they tell a remarkable story.

The Swindon Sunday Mercury in 1996 described the raids of 22 November as, 'Hell on earth. . .In utter devastation, buildings at the centre of Birmingham were smoking shells of their former status. From 7pm came wave after wave of bombers in attacks that would last nine agonising hours. Bombers rained down death and destruction that almost cracked the resolute City.'

The report continued: 'Thousands were left homeless, one hundred and ten factories hit. The railways were crippled, three hundred and seventy sewers were damaged and a thirty-eight-inch gas main was alight. *The three water mains carrying water from the Elan Valley in Wales to Birmingham, were severed and the whole city was left without water apart from that in the canals.*'

Carl Chinn writes in Brum Undaunted: 'At least 682 Brummies were killed during the raids of 19-22 November. Another 1,087 were injured seriously and many more were hurt. These were not the only casualties. No-one has ever found out how many emotions were crushed forever, how many dreams were broken, and how many lives were ruined. The human cost was matched by the destruction of property. Nearly two thousand houses were smashed to pieces and thousands more were damaged seriously.'

The winter of 1940–41 was again exceptionally cold with heavy falls of snow. But throughout the darkening days of winter, night after night, the raids continued.

The longest raid, of thirteen hours, was on the night of 11 December, which started at 6:30 and ended thirteen hours later the following morning. Raids came in three phases, the last starting at 5.30 in the morning just when folk were thinking it was over. Thirteen hours of absolute terror, fires, explosions, death and injury.

I remember that night. After a long day at work, Dad was just about to eat his meal. At half past six the sirens went. . .'woo-ooo-ooo-oohhh.' Rising to a piercing crescendo the sound demanded immediate attention and action, it seemed to scream 'be quick. . .be quick. . .be quick.'

There was a rush of activity and we were hurried into the shelter. It was covered in snow and it was cold. The sound of sirens was normal now, just as it seemed normal to sleep in the shelter. Dad was not on fire duty that night so he was with us. I didn't sleep much and I remember the 'all clear.'

Dad said, 'It's over, they're going away.'

But even as he said it the siren started again. 'wooo'. . .'Oh no,' said Mum, 'not again.'

The destruction continued for a few more hours, the thuds, the whistles and crashes and all the time wondering where it was. I slept fitfully, hearing the low talk and, 'How much longer?' I can't remember feeling afraid. This was what happened at night, it was normal.

Perhaps Dad went out to investigate. He must have wondered if his factory was hit. And then in the early hours, the 'all clear,' came for the second time. The all clear started high and gradually dropped pitch—the dropping pitch seemed to reduce tension.

'We might as well go back to bed and get some sleep,' said Mum, starting to collect things together.' We started to move but yet again the sirens started. I drifted back to sleep and woke hearing the final 'all clear.'

Dad said 'That's it. . .it's over, it really is over this time.' It was 7.30am.

Wearily the day started again. There had not been much sleep that night for any in the city. In many areas, there was no water and gas. Thankfully, throughout those months of the blitz, kettles, pans, jugs and even baths were kept filled with water for just such emergencies.

Dad went off to work. Mum took us to join endless food queues, although many shops were demolished or boarded up. She stood horrified at the destruction and debris in the streets around–so close to home. Gaping houses grotesquely exposed their inner rooms to passers-by; beds hung precariously from collapsing floors, and pictures still hung on walls. Firemen put out smouldering fires in houses, and defused unexploded bombs. Gas leaked from fractured mains.

Winston Churchill had said, 'We will never surrender. . .*we will fight on the streets*.' His words had come true.

9

BLITZ CHRISTMAS 1940

Christmas 1940 was cold and dreary. Dad cleared snow from the path to
the shelter every night. Every night there was more to clear. The shelter
with its corrugated steel walls, covered in wet earth and topped by snow,
got increasingly cold. British rail reported in January that 15 thousand miles
of track were blocked by snow and ice.

In June 1940, the government decided to restrict the supplies of non-
essential consumer goods to the home market. It cut the production of
seventeen classes of consumer goods *to two-thirds of the 1939 level*. This
included toys, jewellery, cutlery and pottery.

In addition, after a year of rationing, housewives had to be inventive in
their cooking. There were hardly enough coupons for a chicken if available
and one shop claimed to have only two turkeys between 56 customers.

There were no Christmas displays in the shops because of blackout.
Many city centre shops had been demolished or were boarded up and
looked black and forbidding. The Bullring Market Hall, where so many
Brummies had 'Christmas shopped,' was flattened. Christmas presents were
home-made—socks, scarves pullovers—often from unravelled wool from
old garments.

Determined to make the best of it, some families decorated their
shelters with streamers and put up stockings for Father Christmas.

In the end it wasn't necessary as there was a truce by both sides from
Christmas Eve to the 29th December and then the raids started again. I
have only one memory of that Christmas when I was three-and-a-half.
Uncle Percy and Aunty Doris lived in the next street and we all went there

on Christmas Eve. I remember being curled up on the settee. The lights were very low and Percy had bright beady eyes that glittered as he told us a ghost story about an old lady he met on the stairs.

'But which stairs,' Percy nodded to the door that led to the small hall and stairs—they were a mirror image of ours. We held our breath and stared at the door, we knew exactly what the stairs looked like. 'But who was she?'

Percy shook his head and his eyes opened wider and glittered even more. 'I don't know but she chased me downstairs with a whip.'

'Did she catch you?' Percy led us on with his story about the old lady but we didn't get any more from him. I suspect Mum or Dad signalled to him to stop. I snuggled closer to Dad, still staring at the door.

The raids continued in the cold weather of February when evacuations started yet again after more water mains were fractured. Large parts of the city were without water for days. Would it ever end? By now Mum and Dad were desperate to get away from the nightly raids. It was unbelievable that they had survived but it was impossible to find anywhere else to rent. So many houses had been damaged or destroyed and homeless families had first priority. We had not been made homeless, we were not a priority; we just lived in a target area.

By the spring of 1941, months of sleeping in damp Andersons or sheltering in crowded public shelters had taken its toll on the nation's health. The Bishop of Birmingham raised anxiety about the increase in infectious diseases. In a debate, in the House of Lords, he said, in the first months of 1941, whooping cough cases had increased, from four thousand the previous year, to 31 thousand. I don't think our shelter was particularly damp but we three girls all caught whooping cough. We whooped our way through whooping cough, followed by chicken pox that spring whilst we were still in Church Street. We all sat together in the big double bed for two or three weeks and we finished by getting German measles. The worst part was the whooping and the difficulty in breathing as well as the coughing and wheezing that seemed endless. It was called the 'hundred-day cough' because the illness lasted for several weeks.

I can't remember if they took us into the shelter in those days when we were ill, but guess they probably just risked staying in the house. Mum talked about the time when they heard the unexpected whistle of a bomb dropping and dived under the table for cover.

There was a tiny fireplace in the bedroom and we thought that if Dad lit the fire, the room would get warm. . .it seemed a good idea. We kept begging, 'Please, Dad light the fire.'

Eventually he did light it once. He carried a shovel of burning coals from the fire downstairs and put it into the fireplace. The room was warm then, but the smoke swirled back into the room instead of up the chimney and made us cough and splutter even more. Of course he had guessed that would happen and that was why he hadn't wanted to light it.

The house was always cold in winter. When it was bedtime, we children didn't want to leave the warmth of the fire to go upstairs to bed.

Mum warmed our nightclothes on the fireguard, 'You can get undressed down here,' she said, 'it's warm by the fire.' That was a treat but we still didn't want to go up to the cold bedroom. 'Quick,' she said, 'up wooden hills,' and we raced upstairs to get into bed as quickly as we could.

'What are wooden hills?

We knew but that was the excuse for her to sing as she tucked us into bed.

'Up wooden hills, down sheet lane, into blanket market and pillow slip fair.' But where was pillow slip fair?. . .I wanted to go there.

There was no heating upstairs and sometimes ice formed on the inside of the windows during the night. When it was really cold she said, 'I'll warm the sheets for you.' She put hot cinders from the fire into a brass warming pan and carried it upstairs. I watched as the hot pan was moved around under the covers. As a child, it seemed a very clever way of bringing heat from downstairs, upstairs. We must have been the last generation to have actually used a warming pan! Later the warming pan was replaced by a stone hot water bottle.

After a few minutes Mum said, 'There, you will soon get warm.' I never felt 'soon', was soon enough. Sheets and blankets were not as cosy as a duvet. It didn't help that the floor was covered with lino. That felt really cold, although there were small mats pegged by Mum from all sorts of bright materials.

On really cold mornings, after Dad got up, we got into bed with Mum. Their bed was always warm and cosy. His first job was to light the fire downstairs and make Mum a cup of tea. We snuggled down in the warmth whilst Dad shivered on the cold lino.

He pulled on his cotton 'Long Johns', a white cotton vest, a starched shirt with a 'button on collar' and trousers held up with braces. Over that came a brightly patterned Fair Isle pullover, knitted by Mum. He was proud of the way he fastened his tie so that it looked immaculate. He said it was his secret way. Last of all he pulled on hand-knitted, three quarter length socks and fumbled to fasten the suspenders just below his knees.

Stamping his feet in the cold; he put on shoes, polished to a bright shine the night before, and finally went downstairs. Mum drank her tea and only then did she get up to cook Dad's breakfast. The bed went cold very quickly without Mum.

There was double summertime during the war years which meant evenings were lighter for longer but blackout was still rigidly enforced. One episode illustrates how seriously it was taken. It was spring and I was nearly four. It was 'blackout dark' in the house when I woke and called for Mum, there was no answer. I got out of bed and remember trying to turn on the landing light— but it didn't work, I called again— then felt my way downstairs. In the back room I tried to turned that light on. The light didn't work and the house was empty.

I started to feel really anxious, 'Mum— Mummy where are you?' It was so dark 'Where are you?'

Then I heard, 'Here in the garden.' What a relief. I opened the door, she was talking to a neighbour. I went out and she picked me up. I was content just listening to the adults chatting.

We stood for a long time until Mum suddenly said, 'Something's burning,' and ran back into the house.

She had been ironing on the table which was covered with a sheet and blanket. The iron was plugged into the overhead light socket—a normal custom at the time. When it got dark, she switched the iron off at the light switch and went outside. When I came downstairs, I switched on the light switch. But that turned the iron on again. Whilst we were outside, the iron burned through several layers of sheets and blankets; there was a deep, charred, black imprint of the iron on the oak surface.

For many years, I had a dream of being in a dark house and going from room to room, trying to turn on a light. I just couldn't get any light to work. In my dream, I feel panic rising. Years later, during a casual conversation with Dad, he commented, 'In the war we took all the light bulbs out of the sockets, apart from one downstairs, in case you girls turned a light on and broke the blackout.' The penny dropped—my dream of not getting lights to come on, was an actual memory. In fact, removing light bulbs, was Government recommendation.

10

THE NIGHT OF A THOUSAND FIRES

After February, the air-raids seemed to ease off but it was a false hope. We moved from Church Street on 9 April, 1941. It is my clearest memory of all; the knock on the door on that dark moonless night.

There were warnings of a massive raid on the City. By now, fifty-one radar bases were in place around the coast of southern Britain; these gave early warning of the approach of German planes. Dad was on fire watch and heard the news. This was going to be a really big raid judging by the number of planes that were heading for Birmingham.

I don't know what he was thinking as he heard the reports, but it must have been that we surely wouldn't survive yet another raid of this proportion. He wasn't even at home with us. Somehow, Dad contacted his brother-in-law, Eddie, and he came to take us out of Church Street.

Eddie banged on the door. Annie let him in as he was saying, 'Be quick, Bill says there's going to be a really big raid tonight; you've got to come to our house.

I remember being hurriedly got out of bed, taken downstairs and dressed. It was probably about 8 pm when we were in the first deep sleep of the night. I was hardly awake and Mum was saying 'Come on hurry.'

She was packing bags and I remember the room was dark and shadowy. She moved like lightening collecting this and that, dressing Ann, helping me.

I was half asleep as I tried to put on some clothes. 'Where are we going?'

'Cherry Orchard, you can go to bed there.'

I recall walking along a road following Uncle Eddie who was carrying

Ann. It seemed an endless walk in the dark night. Aunty Kath's house, was two miles further out of the city.

I couldn't keep up with them, I was not quite four and they seemed to walk so fast. 'Carry me, my legs are aching.' I called.

'I can't Ann needs carrying, she is only little.' My Uncle was carrying her on his shoulders.

'Mummy you carry me.'

She couldn't, she was carrying as many of our worldly possessions as she could in bags and bundles. I remember seeing the weight she was carrying and realising it was pointless to ask again.

It was pitch black, there were no street lights and we had no torches because of the blackout. I remember falling behind in the darkness feeling helpless and tired. I just wanted to sit down. For some reason I remember passing Handsworth Park and trailing my hands along the railings, it was so very dark and looked like a big empty blackness. It was a long walk for a small child woken out of sleep. We never went back to Church Street.

Our walk was on the night of one thousand fires, when Birmingham suffered one of the most vicious of all raids. From 9:30pm, wave after wave of bombers came all through the night from every direction. Heavy explosives and incendiary bombs were dropped across the city on houses and factories and the centre of the City was ablaze again. Damage to water mains was extensive and widespread and again there was a shortage of water.

That night the City Arcade was flattened and the Corn Exchange destroyed. There were direct hits on the Theatre, the Children's Courts and the Coroners Courts, the General Hospital and the Telephone Exchange. The Gas works erupted into a gigantic blaze. Much of High Street and New Street were destroyed. There were one hundred and five deaths in Lozells. German planes dropped more than 650 HE bombs in swathes across every section of the city, causing one thousand fires.

In his Evening Despatch report, Charles Martin wrote after the war: 'On 9 April the battle of the flames was resumed. . .That night there were 1,000 incidents with 11,000 fire wardens on duty. I spent part of that night on the roof of the Evening Despatch building, it was like being in an angry sea of flames. . .Dale End was ablaze, Dalton Street was a furnace. Fire was devouring everything. Morning brought an equally unforgettable sight. The vicious glow of the flames had vanished but the pungent smell of smoke was everywhere. Massive steel girders, twisted into fantastic shapes, were flung across roadways. Water ran from still smouldering heaps of rubble and gave off clouds of steam.

One cannot help marvelling at the fortitude with which the city underwent the horrors of those nights. Nights and days when raw wounds gaped and smoke curled weirdly amongst endless arcades of masonry and twisted steel, when the contours of the city had been battered out of recognition, when each morning saw crowds round casualty lists scanning anxiously for the fate of family and friends.'

My mother had written in September the previous year, 'Still, we are very optimistic and on the whole very cheerful. Nothing matters as long as we are spared. We and England can build again. Everything is possible if we try hard enough.'

Six months later Birmingham had been *'blitzed' almost to the ground*. The City was unrecognisable. The difficulties of clearing bomb sites, presented huge problems and there was still another four years of war to endure. My enduring childhood memory is of bomb sites ringed with barbed wire and of the rampant buddleia and pink rosebay willowherb which flourished on the bare earth. Those plants, first to grow on the rubble, softened sites of destruction giving hope of new life one day.

The Blitz killed over two thousand Birmingham folk and seriously injured another three thousand. The final number of houses destroyed were more than 12 thousand, as well 302 factories and hundreds of other buildings including much of the Civic Centre of the city.

Every available person was involved in the war effort in some way and had been told their work must take priority. Night shift workers stayed at their posts in munitions factories throughout raids. Men had to serve as fire watchers for 48 hours each month, with the instruction that 'protection of workplaces will take precedence over protection of homes.'

Night after night men who were working, or on duty with Civil Defence or fire watching, did not know what was happening to their wives and children. Many times a person arrived home to find their loved ones had been killed in an air raid, or their homes were demolished and families were missing. Many wives didn't know what was happening to their husbands.

I often wonder how Mum and Dad felt knowing, that by now, they should have had their own 'safe' house nearby. But they never grumbled and never said, 'If only.' They were just relieved we were still alive.

11

A PORT IN THE STORM

After our walk through the night of the raid, we stayed with Aunty Kath and Uncle Eddie in Cherry Orchard, whilst Mum and Dad looked for somewhere else to live. It was Easter 1941. That night, was the last significant raid on Birmingham. We had lived in Church Street for five years, the last six months of which were through the worst of the Blitz on Birmingham. It was peaceful in Cherry Orchard. I was four years the month after we moved.

After the house in Church Street, which was cosy but dark, the house in Lloyd Road was light and spacious—a typical 1930s semi. There was a big lounge and a dining room with French windows. It had a lovely 'retro' green and cream kitchen, really modern for the time. As part of the fitments there was a cupboard, with a glass fronted storage space at the top. Below that a door dropped down to form a working surface and revealed more 'secret' places. Underneath were drawers and more cupboards. In the days before streamlined working surfaces, this was a clever way to provide storage.

I was fascinated and pulled the cupboards and drawers open and closed, until I was told, 'Stop opening that cupboard.' I stopped—for a while.

After we moved to Lloyd Road, Dad went to visit his policeman brother in Walsall. Travel was restricted and permission was needed to travel between areas, along with valid identity cards. The Government wanted to know the movements of civilians. Uncle Arnold's work meant he could not talk about it, even to his brother. But he did tell Dad that he was getting married.

When Dad returned, he said to Mary and me, 'Uncle Arnold wants you to be bridesmaids when he gets married.' He was so pleased and continued, 'You're going to have special bridesmaids' dresses and there will be a party with all the family there.'

Aunty Kath said, 'If we pool our coupons I can make dresses for the girls, what do think Annie?' What's a bridesmaid, I thought?

It was May and I was four and Mary seven. Somehow between the families, they found the coupons for our dresses which were floor length apricot taffeta. We wore apricot bonnets lined with pale green ruched satin and tied with a green satin bow and carried baskets of roses. There was a rehearsal the night before in a big old fashioned Methodist church which had a balcony all the way round. We practised walking in and out of the church following the bride.

'Lift up your baskets girls,'—I kept forgetting, it seemed a long time hanging around.

'No that's no good, turn your hand round this way—and lift it up.'

That was really difficult for a four-year-old and mine kept dragging on the floor. 'Lift it up.' I was told repeatedly, I tried so hard but failed. My outstanding memory is worrying about the basket

For special occasions, Mum tied our hair in rags to make ringlets. We had ringlets under those big bonnets. Strips of cloth were bound around sections of hair and twisted tightly round and round. They were left in overnight and tied so tightly that it hurt to lie on them. Next morning, we were little versions of Shirley Temple, the dancing child singer, with masses of blonde curls; she was a child idol of the 1940s. Sometimes Mum achieved the ringlets by using a curling iron heated on the fire. I remember the horrible smell of burning hair from that; and Mum saying 'keep still.'

When Uncle Arnold and his bride came back from honeymoon I went to stay with them for a week. It was wartime and they made me eat rice pudding—which I hated.

'Now, Muriel eat your rice pudding.' I shook my head.

'We can't waste food, it's good for you.'

'I don't like rice pudding.'

'You are lucky to have rice pudding and you'll stay there until you've finished it.'

'Mummy wouldn't make me eat it.' I stopped there for a very long time, sitting at the table on my own.

One day, for the Sunday School Anniversary at Aston Villa Methodist Church, we wore our bridesmaids' dresses again. A big fuss was made of Methodist Anniversaries. It was always a special time when the boys had new shirts and all the girls new dresses. Aunty Kath made us new white dresses every year and carefully stitched old fashioned smocking, across the bodice.

This year there was a 'pageant' for the anniversary and the girls were dressed as flowers. Because our bridesmaid's dresses were gold, we were either daffodils or marigolds. Tiers of bench seats, rising high into the church roof, were specially erected for the occasion. We climbed high up to our seats and I remember all the faces looking at us. I looked instead to the right and out of the roof windows which were now on a level with our seats. We sang the children's songs we had practised and Dad conducted us.

We were only in Lloyd Road for a few months and moved away in the summer. I recently returned and as I stood outside the house, there was an evocative smell of petrol. My mind was immediately catapulted back down the years into Uncle Eddie's garage. It was a treasure trove of interesting objects, equipment, tools, deck chairs and lots of lovely little pots. I could see it in a flash as if I was standing there—a slight smell of petrol and leather and of old fashioned 'bygone' cars. How powerful a smell can be in surfacing memories.

Aunty Kath's house represented a haven of safety and peace after Church Street and Mum and Dad were relieved and more relaxed and we all sensed that

Eddie was a favourite uncle who played with us. Sometimes he sang a song that seemed really strange—'Mairzy doats and dozy doats and liddle lamzy tivey. A kiddley tivey too. Wouldn't you?'

It seemed like a children's' song and we joined in with him not knowing what it meant. Soon we knew it by heart. Later we learned it was, 'Mares eat oats and does eat oats and little lambs eat ivy, a kid will eat ivy too, wouldn't you?' I was so disappointed because I thought Mairzy Doats was a person and I liked the name and it had a swing when sung that way. It didn't matter that it was nonsense.

Another wartime favourite we all sang was 'Run rabbit - run rabbit - Run! Run! Run!' First sung by Flanagan and Allen in 1939 it became popular when they poked fun at Hitler by changing the words to 'Run Adolf, run Adolf, run, run, run.' We children just sang the rabbit song.

> Run rabbit - run rabbit - Run! Run! Run!
> Run rabbit - run rabbit - Run! Run! Run!
> Bang! Bang! Bang! Bang - Goes the farmer's gun.
> Run rabbit - run rabbit - Run! Run! Run!
> Run rabbit - run rabbit - Run! Run! Run!
> Don't give the farmer his fun! Fun! Fun!
> He'll get by without his rabbit pie
> So run rabbit - run rabbit - Run! Run! Run!

Then and now—So far, my story has been about the Blitz but from now on, it is about life as I experienced it in the 1940s. I want to show how different it was for the simplest of reasons. Every-day tasks took longer; shopping and hours of queuing took time and dictated a way of life that is difficult to imagine today.

These days, we take a car to the supermarket and load a trolley with food. In those days there were no supermarkets and there was nowhere to put a 'load' of food. Not many homes had a fridge or freezer for storage. That meant shopping every day and buying only what would keep short term. Meat was stored in a meat safe with a mesh door to keep flies off. Milk, delivered every day, was kept cool in summer by standing in a bucket of water.

Without a freezer there were no food stocks for emergencies—no convenience foods, no frozen vegetables, pies, cakes or fast food—think how many times a day the fridge or freezer is opened—*shopping every day, took hours out of every day.* Today most homes have a washing machine, but in those days, washing by hand took all day. I remember my mother's amazement when, in the 1950s, she bought a spin dryer and got rid of the mangle, and her great delight with a washing machine in the 60s. *Now she could do in two hours, what used to take all day.*

The smoke and grime from coal fires meant rooms needed cleaning every day; today's houses are easier to clean, modern vacuum cleaners are efficient and in some homes dishwashers replace hours of work. Today, standards of comfort have changed—and also expectations of what is normal. Many homes have central heating, often double glazing but in the 1940s it was rare. Shortage of coal meant homes were always cold. We have transitioned from ice on the windows to radiators, and to grants for insulation in the walls; from warming pans, to stone hot water bottles, to rubber hot water bottles, to electric blankets and from blankets to duvets on the beds.

Travel has speeded up. Grandfather's letters took six weeks by sea from Australia—today a plane takes two days. After they emigrated, my Mother never saw her family again—today Skyping is free and immediate and with 24-hour news we 'see' what is happening in those faraway places instantly.

So what was missing from our 1940s home?

Washing machine, electric cooker, electric toaster, electric kettle, fridge, dishwasher, freezer, television, tumble dryer, cake mixer, computer, tablet, mobile phone, hair dryer, electric razor, microwave, cling-film, foil, boxes of tissues, plastic containers for food storage, 24-hour news, Facebook, Twitter, Instagram and a car.

Those weren't the 'good old days' they were just the 'old days' and so much has changed or gone. I want to describe it as it was then, before it disappears from memory.

12

BAYSWATER ROAD

Finally, Dad found a new home for us. We moved out of Aunty Kath's house at the end of the summer in 1941, in time for Mary to start at her third school, she was seven. It was privately rented and a large Edwardian terraced house in Bayswater Road in Birchfields. Mum and Dad would have preferred to go further out but it was difficult to find property to rent. In a letter written the following year, Mum writes, 'We are still waiting for our new house.' So this one was only transitional.

Our new house was attractive and in a wide road which ran down to Canterbury Road School. At last our own home again. We excitedly explored, trying the bells which were in every room—and trying the patience of Mum and Dad. It seems it was built as a genteel residence with a maid in mind—a box in the kitchen indicated which bell had rung. I think someone disconnected the wiring, as the bells soon stopped ringing.

At last we had room to spread. There were four bedrooms, Mary said 'Bags I this one,' claiming the small bedroom. I learned a new expression that meant, 'This is mine.' Mary was older with a bigger vocabulary!

There was a sitting room with a bay window, a small dining room with French windows onto the back garden and a large kitchen with an Aga type range. The air raid shelter this time was in the dining room. It was called a Morrison shelter after Herbert Morrison, the Minister of Home Security. It looked like a steel table, 2 foot six inches high with mesh sides. To me it looked like a cage. I don't think we ever used it in a raid but I climbed under—and thought I wouldn't want to be there if the house collapsed on top.

The garden had lilac trees at the bottom which seemed like a woodland to play in. When the blossom was out, it meant spring was here and summer ahead. It was my birthday time. Even as a child I loved lilac and the pink and white blossom of apple trees, bluebells and the fresh look of new leaves. The myriads of golden dandelions that sprang up in profusion in May seemed to say 'Happy birthday.'

I started school in January 1942, before my fifth birthday in May. Mum wrote in a letter to her friend, 'Muriel goes to school with Mary.' And that is exactly what I thought I was doing, going to school to keep Mary company. No one told me I was going to be there for many more years—I thought I could stop when I got tired. However, I enjoyed the school that I thought I was only visiting. I was ready to go.

Canterbury Road School was an old fashioned Victorian red brick building with two entrances from the Infant playground. One had 'GIRLS' engraved in stone over the door and the other had 'BOYS.' When the whistle blew at playtime, we lined up at the correct door and waited until everyone was in line and then filed quietly in.

In the playground we played games with the teacher. Holding hands in a circle for Farmer's in his Den, and lining up to make an arch for Oranges and Lemons—singing, chasing and capturing each other with lots of squeals and laughter. In the classroom after playtime, the teacher said, 'Now cross your arms on your desks and put your heads down on your arms. You are going to have ten minutes rest.'

I first learned at that school about the division of sexes. Coming from a home of four girls, including Mum, I'd had little contact with boys to that point. I discovered that boys, who after all, were made of slugs and snails and puppy dogs tails, tore around playgrounds, fought each other, had grazed knees and their socks were always half down. Girls however, played nice games of mummies and daddies, hospitals and nurses. They had nice dolls and played nice dressing up games. After all they were made of sugar and spice and all that's nice.

At some time 'Just William' came into our lives. He was an OK boy. We rushed home from school to listen to the antics of scruffy William and his friends on the wireless at 4pm. Then there was Violet Elizabeth Bott, who always threatened William, 'I'll thcream and thcream 'till I'm thick' (sick) unless she got her own way. Why did she have to let the girls down?

My Victorian classroom had very high ceilings and large high windows. On the walls were the days of the week and weather charts made by children. . .today is Friday and it is raining etc. There were lots of pictures with descriptions by the side. There was a nature table with interesting things including frog spawn and jam jars with beans growing on blotting paper.

On Friday afternoon we played with toys and there was a big red Post Office van that I just loved. The door opened and it was filled with tiny brown paper parcels and letters with tiny stamps. The teacher told us that there was nothing inside the parcels, we must not open them. I knew she was wrong; they were fairy letters and parcels with surprises inside that she didn't know about. Secretly I opened one and to my disappointment there was nothing inside but paper. I still knew there was something in *one* of them but I didn't dare open another.

When I moved up into the next class we sat in rows of desks and there was a big blackboard on an easel at the front. And joy of joys—a book corner. Our first reading book was about the three Billy Goats Gruff and their adventures. I never did like that book but I did love the stories about Ameliaranne and the Green Umbrella, and Milly-Molly-Mandy books.

Ameliaranne Stiggins and her five brothers and sisters, were invited to a party. But because her brothers and sisters were ill, she went to the party on her own. Kind Ameliaranne smuggled cakes and jelly, all mixed up together, in her green rolled umbrella to take home for them. But on the way home—she put up the umbrella in the rain and all the food fell out. Breath catching suspense for a child of five! I really identified with Ameliaranne because, like me, she wore her hair in rags to make ringlets and I knew just how painful that was.

And as for Milly-Molly-Mandy; 'Once upon a time there was a little girl …This little girl had short legs and short striped frocks. But her name wasn't short at all. It was Millicent, Margaret Amanda. Milly Molly Mandy for short.' Nice girly books, just right for nice little girls—and she wore frocks not dresses.

The line between reality and fantasy is blurred in a child's perception. I had a good imagination but it was nothing compared with that of a boy in my class who kept telling me that he had a lake in his garden with a bridge over it; and a swan that he went for rides on. He went to such fascinating places on the swan's back. He kept talking about it and so I kept asking. In the end I made up my mind to investigate this amazing phenomenon. I was nearly six and the roads were safe in those days, so without telling anyone, I set off to find his house.

When I was a child I thought as a child … running down Normandy Road to the place where he lived, I felt so excited. I was going to wonderland, where children rode on swans to faraway places and had adventures . . .perhaps I too would go. I knocked on his door and he took me into the garden.

I was so, so disappointed, the garden was no bigger than ours. 'Well where is the lake?' I said.

'There,' pointing to the tiniest fish pond imaginable. I admit it did have a miniature imitation bridge over it. I stared and stared.

'Well where is the swan?'

'There,' said he, pointing to a concrete duck sitting on the edge of the pond.

'You can't ride on that,' I declared.

With that he sat on the duck and jogged up and down. Again I was so, so disappointed, I felt confused it had seemed so real , but then I was a child and I thought as a child.

Also in my class, was the 'red boy.' At least he always seemed to look red. He wore a red blazer and had a red face but he had white hair.

One day he said to me, 'I'm going to marry you.'

I was so scared. I thought that if he said so, he must know something I didn't, and that he must have some sort of power over me. I didn't want to marry him. Especially as he had a funny name which I can't repeat—I didn't want to be 'Mrs Funny name'. I thought my fate was sealed until I told Dad and was so relieved when he said it wasn't true. It was OK, I was going to marry Dad after all.

In July 1943, there was an unexpected raid after nearly a year's lull. Many incendiary bombs and delayed action bombs were dropped. The next morning, Mary and I skipped to school around the craters left by incendiary bombs. There were six of them down the centre of the road—mini craters, each about five foot across and three foot deep and cordoned off.

We stopped to look at each of them and arrived at school to find yet more craters in the school playground. There was also a massive steam roller parked in the corner of the playground. It was absolutely enormous and frightening. The big roller at the front towered many feet above me—I used to have dreams of it chasing me. It was parked there for a long time and that meant I kept seeing it every day.

We had a special friend who lived next door. At least to us, he seemed more like a friend than a cat. He was called Tinker, also known as Tinkerbelle, and belonged to our neighbour. He was always waiting by the back door in the morning. When we knocked on the window, he looked up and meowed. In fact, he meowed until Dad opened the door and then he shot upstairs to us. We played with him for hours—we dressed the struggling cat in dolls clothes and put a bonnet on him. Then holding him down in the pram, still struggling, we covered him with blankets. But in two or three steps he escaped and ran off wearing the clothes, with us chasing, shrieking and squealing. He always came back for more.

Mum did her shopping on Birchfield Road which was a ten-minute walk away. One place that always fascinated us was Birchfield Odeon 'Picture House' as it was called. I remember standing near the exit and listening to the sounds and looking through whenever the door opened. I was desperate to go in. Eventually we were taken to see Bambi, after that we went to see the Wizard of Oz and sang the songs over and over again, 'Follow the yellow brick road, 'Somewhere over the rainbow bluebirds fly.'

In those days, performances were continuous. You paid to go in at any time and could sit there all day. Two films were always shown, with the news and cartoons between. Picture houses were often the warmest places to pass the hours when the weather was cold.

They were always thick with the fog of cigarettes. Each seat had an ash tray on the back for the use of the person sitting behind. The film was projected from the back and the beam of light shone onto a screen at the front of the cinema. The beam cut through rising smoke and the dust in the air sparkled in the beam. Many times the film reel snapped at a crucial point and everyone complained loudly until it was repaired.

At the end of the day, after the last film ended, the National Anthem was played and everyone stood up and sang 'God Save the King'. For many years the national anthem was also played on television before it closed for the day around 10pm. It was a strange feeling wondering whether to stand up in your own home, so ingrained was the habit. But eventually one realised no-one was watching and both habit and practice died.

There was a ladies' hairdresser near the picture house. One day, Mum sent us with Mary, who was nine and very practical and could do anything, to have our hair cut. Mary and Ann went in but I was lagging quite a long way behind. When I got there, I went into the Barber's next door by mistake. Without asking any questions, he sat me on a high stool and cut off all my hair. I watched with horror as my hair came off and I was too young to question or stop him. I thought, even at that age, how ugly my hair looked. In those days a boy's hair cut was 'short back and sides,' and that's what I finished up with. I was wearing a dress so why couldn't he see I was a girl?

Mary came in and paid the Barber but she didn't ask why I had been there and not with them. I was crying and really upset.

'Whatever's the matter.' Mum said.

'The man cut my hair off, I wanted it like Mary's.'

'Well where *did* you go?'

'She went next door.' Mary answered.

'Oh into the barber's, well never mind it will grow again.'

But I felt something irrevocable had happened to me. I was still upset and went into the bathroom to see my ugly new look. I looked for a long time in the mirror. And then I found a pair of scissors in the bathroom. I knew that ladies plucked their eyebrows, it was the fashion to have high black pencilled arches and I thought I would look better with my eyelashes off. With great precision I cut them off.

'Look Mum.' I showed them to her, 'I cut my eye lashes.'

'Whatever have you done,' she panicked, 'You could have blinded yourself, ladies don't cut off their lashes.' Now I had no eye lashes and no hair. . .or at least very short hair.

As the war progressed rationing got even more stringent. In April 1943 Mary was nine and she had her first ever birthday party. Mary was so thrilled and knew exactly who she wanted to invite. Her friend from down the road came and some friends from school. Mum had to save rations for several weeks to get enough for the food.

I can only guess what there was to eat but it was wartime and sandwiches would have been jam or fish paste and possibly egg and cress. Shippams Fish paste, or potted meat was a universal standby and came in small ribbed jars. After that came jelly and pink blancmange followed by fairy cakes and Mum's fabulous jam tarts. Tea was always rigidly ordered, sandwiches first, then jelly and only then cakes. Then party games, probably blind man's bluff, pass the parcel and musical chairs. No crisps, no fizzy pop, no ice cream, no party bags but lots of fun.

A month later Mum wrote to her friend, 'Mary had a lovely time at her party with ten little girls and boys.' she also said 'It's Muriel's birthday tomorrow and she wants a party but can't have one because I haven't got enough fats, I had to save for weeks for Mary's party.'

We were all treated the same but sometimes circumstances made a difference as it did here. To save for weeks to get enough margarine to make a cake, indicates just how small the rations were. I was really disappointed about the party and I don't think I ever had one as a child.

Nevertheless, I remember on my birthday skipping to school. I met a neighbour and said 'It's my birthday today, I'm six.'

'Happy birthday Muriel', he said. I went on skipping—I was always skipping—saying 'It's my birthday today and I'm six', to everyone I met.

In February 1943, Mum wrote to her friend that she and Dad had been to see the film 'The Great Mr. Handel' which was in Technicolour. She said that the singing was wonderful and they both wanted to join in. A film with sound and colour only sixteen years after the first talking films in 1927. The film must a classic because it is still available today as a DVD. Dad enjoyed it so much that he went to hear Handel's 'Messiah' sung by the City of Birmingham Choir in the Town Hall. He was very impressed and decided to join the choir. He had a lovely bass voice and really enjoyed singing.

Dad often sang to us and told us silly rhymes and played on the floor with us and walked with a silly walk, deliberately falling over to make us laugh, long before Basil Fawlty.

A favourite place Dad often took us to was Aston Hall. The soot blackened, Gothic building with its many towers, seemed mysterious and exciting. Was there really a secret corridor hidden behind the bench in the hall? And surely there must be a treasure hidden somewhere in that ornate chest with all those drawers? We were actually allowed to open the drawers, only to discover more secret doors and hiding places behind.

We heard about King Charles I staying at the Hall and how it was attacked in the Civil War. We held the heavy cannon balls and stared at the cannon gun and tried to imagine the battle in the Park. Meanwhile a barrage balloon floated overhead in defence against a different type of bomb.

I hadn't seen Aston Hall since childhood but when I returned recently, I was as thrilled as ever. It was open after three years of restoration costing £12 million. The blackened brickwork is cleaned of centuries of soot and grime. The interior refurbished and the magnificent paintings and ceilings restored. The wonderful oak staircase has been restored as well as the incredible panelling. What an amazing city treasure.

Built in 1618 by Sir Thomas Holte, a Royalist supporter of Charles I, it was home for the Holte family for two hundred years. It has belonged to Birmingham City since the 1850s when it was the first museum of its kind in the country.

At some time in 1941, Dad started to work for Birmingham Housing Management Department. As a Council 'estate agent' his job involved helping to re-house the thousands of families whose homes were blitzed. He looked after Council tenants, dealt with property repairs and complaints, and collected rents.

Not long before moving to Birmingham, Dad applied with his brother to join the Police Force but he was just ½ inch too short, rules were rigidly applied in those days. His six-foot brother was accepted. Dad was rejected and was so disappointed. It was one of many disappointments in his life. Because his father died when he was eight, he reluctantly left school at thirteen. His mother was a widow and he was the oldest boy. He needed to work to help support the family. It was also WWI, and there were few opportunities for him. He really wanted to learn so he went to evening classes to further his education. He taught himself to play the piano, taught himself carpentry and DIY—things his father would have taught him. He vowed his girls would get the schooling he missed.

He settled happily into his new job but still had to continue fire watching in a local factory. He was working for the City Council when Mum wrote to a friend in February 1943, 'There is an ARP outpost on the factory where Bill fire watches and one person, who was traced to there, was caught signaling whilst a raid was on.

Spies and talk of spies both real and fictitious was rampant and many spies were caught and interned. Throughout the war, a British traitor, William Joyce also known as Lord Haw-Haw, broadcast messages from Germany. The aim was to spread Nazi propaganda and undermine morale in Britain. The broadcasts always began with the words 'Germany calling, Germany calling.' To the listener it sounded like an affected: 'Jairmany calling, Jairmany calling.' He gained the nickname 'Lord Haw-Haw' because of the affected way he spoke.

Most of the time, he was listened to with amusement, but sometimes he caused panic with accurate descriptions of places in Britain and events that were happening. Joyce was a British Fascist and admired Hitler. He was hanged as a traitor in 1945.

Because of spies there was a ban on the use of binoculars and telescopes in coastal areas. That ban was lifted by the War Minister the day after war ended. Another ban that was lifted on the same day, was the restriction on weather forecasting. There were no weather forecasts broadcast from the day war was declared—the enemy could use the information to advantage for raids. The day after war ended, the Birmingham Mail reported that all censor restrictions had been lifted and 'For the first time since the start of the war it is possible to tell the world what weather Britain is having whilst having it.'

13

HARD TIMES

There were fewer raids now and in 1941 we settled into a long period of increased austerity. Blackout made everyone feel miserable, particularly in the long dark nights of winter. Food shortages increased and clothes bought before the war, were beginning to wear out.

Working hours in the factories were long and hard. From 1940 'Music while you Work' was broadcast live every day to British factory workers, to increase wartime productivity and boost morale. By the end of the war, 5 million workers in over 9 thousand factories were tuning in across the country.

Another programme along these lines was 'Worker's Playtime' which was broadcast live on the BBC Home Service. It was always introduced as, 'Worker's Playtime from a factory canteen somewhere in Britain.' It was a touring show which the BBC transported with a producer and crew, plus variety artists, up and down the country three times a week until 1957. During the war it was not allowed give the venue—and as people enjoyed the mystery and the guessing where it was, that 'mystery' remained when the programme continued after the war.

Female factory workers wore turbans to cover their hair to prevent accidents with machinery. They looked attractive and were also useful to cover the curlers often worn underneath. Princess Elizabeth started a fashion for wearing a headscarf and that became very popular. The fashionable style for hair, was in a roll at the back and swept up at the front.

Clothes in wartime seem particularly drab in my memory. Probably because of shortage of material and coupons, all the women seemed to wear the same drab dark coats which were straight and economical in use of material. A hat was always worn when outside and they all looked the same too—head hugging felt with brims. A woman would feel undressed without a hat, it just wasn't done. There are many wartime pictures of women all dressed the same, waiting in the inevitable long queues.

Raw materials were in short supply during the war so clothing was rationed by coupons from June 1941. Coupon allowance was sixty-six per person, per year, which would buy one complete outfit of clothing for an adult. Government regulations controlled how much cloth could be used in a garment. Pockets were restricted, the length of dresses were specified. The fashion for women during wartime was sensible low heeled shoes, because they had to last, short skirts and square shouldered jackets. In 1942, Greys Department Store were advertising ladies' dresses for seven coupons and £2-2s-9d.

Rayon and silk stockings with a seam up the back were normal, but it was a struggle to get the seam straight at the back. When it was impossible to get stockings, women sometimes painted stockings on their legs using gravy browning and then drew a line with black eyebrow pencil where the seam was supposed to be. What a pity they didn't have 'fast tan' in those days.

In the days before tights and suspender belts, I remember my mother struggling to put on her pink corset every day. Poor thing. How else could she keep stockings up apart from the suspenders attached to the corset. It was pink, reinforced, and fastened with endless hooks and eyes down the front and extended from underneath the bust to the tops of the thighs. There was nothing glamorous about this underwear. These women were only one generation away, from the women who had worn tightly laced corsets and bustles. Later suspender belts of a sort could be bought. Some younger women managed to get parachute silk and that was used to make more glamorous underwear.

My mother was only thirty-eight in 1940 but that generation seemed older, earlier. They were totally different from the glamorous young mums of today. Christian names were rarely used and even next door neighbours spoke to each other using surnames—'Mrs Brown or Mrs Black' etc.

We girls wore dresses, or frocks, that were short above the knee with pretty puffed sleeves and short white ankle socks. Like any other girl, we invariably had a bow in our hair which Mum always carefully tied and arranged. Our dresses were often smocked on the bodice down to the waist and then gathered. We looked like the Enid Blyton illustrations of our time.

In the winter, when it was cold, we wore 'liberty bodices' over our vests to keep us warm. They were fleece lined and buttoned down the front and had four suspenders to keep stockings up. We needed those bodices. There was no central heating in most houses, and winters seemed colder. Mum also knitted leggings for us to wear outside. Sometimes we had fleecy lined gaiters—those were like leggings but were buttoned down the side using a little hook that pulled the button though a loop.

Boys wore short grey flannel trousers until they were thirteen. To limit material, men's' and boy's jackets could only have three buttons and two pockets. Dad re-soled our shoes using an old fashioned shoe 'last' and sometimes put studs in the soles of his own shoes to make them last longer. A shoe last was a metal form, with three different sizes of 'feet' that could hold different sizes of shoes. Today they are vintage and often used as door stops.

'Make do and mend' was the slogan of the day. Clothes were recycled continuously into many changes of garments. They were patched and adapted, swapped and handed down. Frayed collars and cuffs were unpicked and turned 'outside in'. We girls had to learn to darn socks held in place on a little wooden mushroom — neatly weaving the threads side to side and up and down. It must have been difficult with three growing children to clothe on limited clothes coupons. Mum often used her old treadle sewing machine to adapt the hand downs. She did everything at full speed and it was mesmerising watching her feet pound the treadle as the needle shot up and down.

Whatever was finally discarded, was 'pegged' into rugs or mats for the floor. It was fascinating watching a mat grow from all sorts of old material in lots of colours.

Mum knitted endlessly. Cardigans, bonnets, jackets and leggings, baby clothes and blankets, she was always making something. One fashion was the patterned 'Fair Isle' waistcoats or jumpers—often using coloured scraps of wool rescued from discarded garments. Another was the 'pixie hoods' she knitted for us. We girls were taught to knit socks on four needles and learned how to 'turn a heel', or to knit scarves or gloves and mittens. These tasks were expected 'life skills' for girls in those days.

If it was bought new, wool was in 'skeins' or 'hanks' which meant huge bundles that needed to be wound into balls.

'Help me with this wool,' said Mum, 'Hold your hands apart.'

I stretched them out about eighteen inches apart and she looped one end of the hank of wool over one wrist and another over the other wrist. She then wound the wool into a ball. Often the wool got tangled and took ages to patiently unravel and sometimes a knot mysteriously appeared.

'Oh don't bother, I will cut that out,' But I liked the job of 'unknotting'. I liked the challenge and would sit for ages.

If you couldn't make do and mend, there was the 'Black Market' in foods and clothes for those determined to bypass the regulations. Food, clothing and a range of items could always be bought at a price. The black market supplied 'Under the counter goods.' This meant goods in short supply were kept away from display and only made available to special customers. Those customers would usually pay more for goods, regardless of the Law or regulations of trade. 'Spiv' or 'wide boy' was a word that was coined in wartime and represented the person who made a living by various disreputable dealings, rather than holding down a job, He had 'contacts' for supplying black market illegal goods.

Marguerite Patten, author of many cookery books during and after the war, advised the Government on British wartime diet. Advice and recipes were printed on labels, in newspapers and government recipe books. Many recipes were really inventive and some of them sound strange. Eggs were rationed but dried eggs were available on ration. One tablespoon of dried egg powder was mixed with two tablespoons of cold water and when mixed thoroughly could be used in cakes and omelets etc.

Woolton Pie was recommended as wholesome balanced food by Lord Woolton, the food minister. The pie, invented by the Chef de Cuisine at the Savoy Hotel in London, was vegetarian, quite tasty and served in British kitchens. It was made with 1 lb each of diced, potatoes, cauliflower, swede and carrots, 3 spring onions plus 1 tablespoon of oatmeal. Simmer all together for ten minutes, put into a pie dish, add any available herbs and top with pastry or potato. I had a go at making this recently and it tasted great with some extra herbs.

Mum complained in the winter about the amount of mud on the potatoes.

'Look at this,' she pointed to the potatoes she was peeling. 'lumps of mud and there is more mud than potato.' She often said the same, 'I've paid for all this mud, and a lot of the potato is black inside.' This happened in a cold winter when the potatoes were dug up from frosty ground.

'How can I make this into a meal, I haven't got anymore.'

'Well we could have potato fritters'. So the problem was solved. Thin slices of potato were dipped into batter and deep fried. They were delicious.

The greengrocer wouldn't let anyone choose their own fruit and vegetables, you had what was given you. Potatoes weren't washed for the customer to pick and choose.

In spite of rationing, Mum was a good cook and somehow she rustled up lovely meals and made delicious cakes. Tins of spam were always available, so she made Spam fritters, coated in batter and deep fried. Similarly, delicious apple fritters deep fried and tossed in sugar were favourites. I never remember Mum weighing anything or following a recipe. She learned to cook presumably from her own mother.

Grandad sent food parcels in the war. One day just before Christmas a parcel arrived.

'Whatever is that?'

The brown wrapping came off a box which contained some brown shriveled pieces of 'something' which looked very unappetising.

Mum was overjoyed, 'Its fruit from Dad's farm.' she said.

'Ughh, it looks horrid, not like fruit.'

'It's dried fruit. . .apples, apricots and pineapple grown on his farm.'

When I saw it I thought it would taste like it looked—horrid, but when I tried a small rubbery bit it tasted sweet and chewy and nice after all.

Mum was overjoyed to have something to make puddings, in the days of hardship. Some of Grandad's letters and parcels took as long as four months to arrive during the war because of the danger and delays on the seas.

Soap and toilet paper began to be in short supply. There was an awful wartime toilet paper called Izal. It was on a roll and like very, very thin hard greaseproof paper. In time, even that was difficult to get and people resorted to tearing newspaper into squares and hanging it in the toilet. In fact everything was in short supply and became expensive. Queuing for food is a vivid part of my childhood memories. Someone said 'If there is a queue, join it because something is available.' Eventually queues became a social activity where news was exchanged.

Uncle Eddie had served in the First World War but he was exempt in the second. All men between 18 and 41 were liable for conscription into the armed forces but a list of 'Reserved Occupations' had been drawn up. Exemptions covered five million men in a vast range of jobs including Uncle Eddie's business, which was a small engineering firm.

Another group not drafted into military service, was the 'Bevin Boys.' At the beginning of the war, the Government conscripted coal miners into the armed forces. Eventually it was realised that this resulted in a shortage of properly qualified miners. In the winter of 1943, Britain became desperate for coal, both for home use and for the war effort.

Ernest Bevin, who was Minister of Labour and National Service, announced that 10 per cent of new conscripts to the forces would be sent to the mines. The Bevin Boys worked in the coal mines from December 1943 until 1948 and were chosen at random from those called up for National Service. They came from differing professions and were given six weeks training before working in the mines. For many, working in cold dark mines was a shock and very different from what they were used to. They were not recognised for their contribution to the war, until Tony Blair informed the House of Commons in June 2007, that thousands of Bevin Boys would receive an honour and a Veterans Badge.

During the war the cost of defence and of providing and supplying armed forces was phenomenal. There were big drives to collect money through Government sponsored Savings Bonds or Stamps and Certificates which were sold with a promise of return with interest after the war. Communities and cities were encouraged to compete against each other to raise the most money.

Every child had a Post Office savings box given to them at school and they were shaped like small books in different colours. Mine was green. There was a grill to push cash through and a hole to put a rolled up note through. It was impossible to empty them without taking them to the Post Office. I remember desperately trying to get the money out of the grill at the top with a knife, it was my money, I thought; I didn't want to put it into a savings book.

The Post Office was still charging 2½d for a first class postage stamp, anywhere in the UK, that would arrive the next day by first post. Second-class stamped letters still sometimes arrived the next day. There were two deliveries each day.

We were still at Canterbury Road School when Mum wrote, 'The girls' school had a big effort for 'Wings for Victory' savings week. Every day they had to take savings and Bill finished the week for them and bought them each a certificate. They had nine between them.' I don't know where we got the money to take every day; I assume Dad supplied it all anyway. She said, '*Birmingham collected 16 million pounds for 'Wings for Victory' during that week.* That was a huge amount for war wearied people.

14

THE GREAT BRITISH TRAIN

Before writing these recollections, I didn't understand the vital role of the British railways in wartime and that the country could not have survived without them.

Those of us who remember the war will remember the trains we travelled on. We remember uniformed servicemen, and crowded swaying trains chuffing through the English countryside. We remember billowing smoke and the guard's whistle; pictures of faraway places and misty gas lit platforms with romantic names.

The music of Paul Temple's Coronation Express, captures perfectly the ethos of the time. Jack Adrian, writing an obituary for Francis Durbridge, the author of Paul Temple, wrote the following words: 'Just a hint of the first few bars of Coronation Express, Dur –de –dur –de –de –de –de –de – dur, is enough to transport anyone over the age of fifty to another world.' That is so very true but the reality in wartime was very different.

On 1 September, 1939, the Government took control of all ten privately owned railways. In the following pages, I have included selected paragraphs from the official Wartime Railway report for 1943. They tell a fascinating story that is rarely heard—one that my own words could not express as well as the official record.

There are some staggering facts about transport. Massive numbers needed to be transported on a daily basis. The railways increased their service, in one year, from 325 million to 400 million—an increase of 75 million journeys. The report outlines the following quotes:

'Guns and Armour—the raw materials to make the munitions of war, are all carried on the railways. Loads ranging from the heaviest naval guns and tanks to the lightest rifles and pieces of equipment are rolling along the railways. Aircraft, petrol and fuels; ammunition, bombs, mines, shells and foodstuffs. Vast tonnages of high explosives have been handled through the railways' freight services—and thousands upon thousands of tons of dangerous goods have been safely conveyed.

War Factories—Railways have assisted in the construction of new factories. Bricks and building supplies were conveyed as fast as they could be absorbed. Sidings were laid into fields, signal boxes built, new factory stations erected and services arranged. *Seven thousand additional trains are being run every week* to convey workers to and from Government factories.

Air Raid damage and Repairs—Railway trains, stations and tracks, which are objectives for enemy air raiders, have suffered damage, but the restoration of communications is everywhere rapidly carried out. *As fast as the enemy puts down his high explosives or incendiaries, or shoots up engines and trains, railway engineers tackle the job of making repairs.*

Amongst the achievements of the railways rapid repair organisations are the renewal of main line tracks within a few hours and the restoration of damaged bridges in one day.

A signal box of 68 levers, destroyed by a direct hit, was replaced by a new box next day, including a new mechanical interlocking frame, and within two weeks all the points and main line signals at a busy station were again in operation. In another instance a signal box was repaired within 17½ hours. *Three thousand signal wires were repaired in one week, and six hundred electric cables in eight days.*

At one town, bombs hit a station building, severed four through lines and damaged a train. Almost before the noise of the explosions and falling masonry had ceased, work was resumed. The 'Shuttle' services of buses were arranged *within 15 minutes*; newspapers, mails, milk, fish and other perishable traffics were diverted, and engineers were hard at work clearing the debris to restore the tracks. The damaged train was removed in a few hours, and within 24 hours, a load of steel plates for shipment, was delivered without delaying a ship, passenger train services being resumed within 48 hours after the raid.

Food and fuel—The zoning of supplies, district by district, to make each area of the country as self-supporting as possible, has meant the re-arrangement of hundreds of freight services. The increase of home-grown food, with millions of acres of land under cultivation, is resulting in increasing demands for railway transport. Fertilisers, seed potatoes, sugar beet, tractors and farming equipment, as well as land workers, have been catered for by special trains from the nearest port or primary sources of supply.

Coal. This is no longer carried by coast vessels. Four million tons weekly is carried by the rail.

Air Raid Precautions—fire-fighting organisations of the British railways have been extended: 170 thousand railway employees have received full training in ARP duties. Shelters are provided and forty-seven specially equipped cleansing vans, which can be moved to any station or depot for decontamination, have been located at convenient places for immediate use in the event of gas attacks.

Ambulance Trains—British railways have completed a number of Ambulance Trains for use both at home and overseas. The Ambulance. Trains are fully equipped with furnished cars for travelling staffs of nurses and doctors; kitchens and wards for stretcher, sitting-up and mental cases, and cars are also provided for infectious cases and for travelling pharmacies. The Casualty Evacuation Trains are electrically lighted, steam heated, and are fitted with bell communication and numerous other devices adopted by co-operation with medical authorities to ensure the comfort of patients.

Air raids—Trainmen and signalmen remain at their posts and tickets are issued at the booking offices during air raid warnings. All staff continue at work during air raids until danger is imminent in the immediate vicinity of the places at which they are working, and work is resumed again as soon as the immediate danger is past.

When Under Private Ownership

Travel by passenger train was, in the pre-war years, quick, cheap and comfortable. *Penny-a-mile tickets,* introduced in 1934, were a great success, while the range of other cheap tickets for both individual and party travel was continually being expanded. It was possible to travel by specified excursion trains for as little as a penny for three miles. The variety of cheap tickets was such, that practically all travelers could find something.'

There is more. The whole report makes fascinating reading and can be bought or downloaded online from various sources under 'Facts About British Railways In Wartime 1943.' The copyright is not traceable but the report finishes with, *'Any of the facts and figures given in this book may be quoted with or without acknowledgement. Passed for publication by the Censor.'*

15

WARTIME CHRISTMAS

Every year during the war, Mum and Dad said there won't be much for Christmas. But the same was said in every home. Christmas was always wonderful, it meant being with the extended family. There was always someone to play Ludo or Snakes and Ladders and we played endless games of Snap or Happy Families with patient adults. We sang carols as Dad played the piano and stayed up very late, curled up by the fire, listening to the same stories retold every year. I remember one year learning 'Silent Night' at school. I loved it and sang it for Mum and Dad and told them that the Germans were singing it as well. Of course they already knew.

We decorated our classrooms at school with the paper chains we laboriously made and couldn't wait to put decorations up at home.

'Can we put them up now?' we pleaded

'Not yet but soon.'

Finally, with great excitement, the box was opened.

'Where is he?' We looked first for the jolly red 'Father Christmas'. He had rosy cheeks, a merry smile, curly white hair and a beard and hung on the wall for as long as I remember.

'Dad will you help us put these up?' Red and green garlands were strung around the room.

Finally, out of the decorations box came a flat pack that opened up into a red tissue honeycomb bell, this was suspended from the light. All red and green—and then the room looked 'Christmassy'. *Very unsophisticated* by today's standards but gave colour and excitement in the austere days of war. There were no twinkling sets of lights around the room; homes were dark because of the restricted lighting but we still put up a little Christmas tree. We decorated it with shimmering, glass baubles. They looked so pretty as they reflected the firelight. The colours were beautiful and the ornaments very fragile and easily broken. I can't believe it, but we used tiny *real* candles in holders clipped to the tree. They looked like twisted red sticks of barley sugar. They never stood vertical and leaned at precarious angles however hard we tried to fix them. How dangerous it seems now.

In many ways, the essence of Christmas was the same as today and meant family time. But no TV. . .no mobiles. . .no computer games. . .no vast sums of money spent on children. . .no anxiety about buying the latest craze.

What do you want for Christmas?

'Books and a doll and drawing things, I said.

'Books and a doll and drawing things.' said Ann.

'The same,' said Mary, 'But especially books.'

'I'll do what I can, I think I can get you books but they won't be new.' Dad said the same every year. Paper was restricted for book printing, so people exchanged or bought second hand books from each other. It was the same in every home, where recycled or home-made presents challenged ingenuity. The stores were empty of Christmas goods. Shop fronts were blacked out—no Christmas displays, money was short anyway, in the highly taxed years of war.

But for us it was always, books, drawing things, dolls. Dad invariably managed to find precious books, we didn't mind second-hand as long as we had books. Beatrix Potter, Winnie the Pooh, Enid Blyton we read and re-read them all. One year, the favourite was Tanglewood Tales, stories about ancient Greek mythology by Nathaniel Hawthorne. And then there were science books and general knowledge books. All very different from today's taste.

For a few years I wanted a Rupert Bear Annual which was published by the Daily Express newspaper. It was so popular that during the war, even with the paper shortage, special permission was given by the Government to continue printing it. I remember Dad saying one year, 'I know what Muriel wants, she wants a Rupert Annual—and she shall have one.'

Rupert's red jumper and yellow scarf signalled adventure for a while. As we got older there were lots of other annuals, Blackie's Children's Annual and the Girls Crystal Annual—too many books to remember in spite of the shortages. Dad was so pleased when he got what we wanted. We couldn't get enough to read.

Boys were reading, Knockout and Beano, Boy's Own, Champion Annual, Biggles stories, Arthur Ransome books. They were making models from Meccano, collecting Dinky cars and Hornby Train Sets.

I remember one year we all got a kaleidoscope. 'But what is it?' Dad showed us how to twist the end and look at the magic of tumbling colours and changing patterns. Even today I find the constant variety and beauty breath-taking in such a simple thing. And then there were magic paint books with colour and pictures that magically appeared with a paintbrush and water.

One year, Dad took each of us aside and said, 'What's your favourite colour?'

'Red.' I wanted to know why but he just looked mysterious.
He had made us each a doll's cot and painted it in our favourite colour. Our old dolls were in the cots but covered in new bed clothes which Mum had made. Another toy he made, was a man climbing up a stick and flipping over at the top. Simple but enthralling toys in a simpler age.

One year a parcel of magazines came from relatives on Vancouver Island. I looked with fascination at Christmas in Canada, the Christmas decorations, the 1940s adverts and the pictures of skating on frozen lakes. I can see the pictures now. *I made up my mind, even then, that I wanted to travel to those exciting places and eventually I did.*

In Summer 1944, we moved to Yardley Wood. Aunty Kath then bought the house we rented in Bayswater Road and moved there. I don't know why she wanted to move from Cherry Orchard. Maybe she preferred the older Edwardian style house, which had been built in 1909. Perhaps to her, it had more character, it had obviously been a 'genteel' residence. Maybe the owners wanted to sell it and we had to move out. When Aunty Kath moved in, they removed the Morrison shelter and modernised the house and lived there for a number of years. After that, we always went back for Christmas.

Not long before Christmas, Mum and Dad said very clearly, 'Don't look in the wardrobe in our bedroom.' It was asking for rebellion.

They repeated the same instruction a little later. 'Don't look in the wardrobe in our bedroom.' Something was going on.

When Mary said 'Come and see what's in the bedroom,' we raced upstairs. We opened the door of the wardrobe and there on the top shelf, peeping over the edge, in fact almost dropping off, were three dolls.

'Oh' I said, 'I hope I get that one,' pointing to a big blonde doll, 'She's got eyes that open and close.' There was a pretty brown haired doll and I think there was a baby doll. Surprisingly we each wanted a different one. I had been asking for a doll with eyes that opened and closed for a long time.

Christmas arrived, and Christmas Eve was a long and sleepless night waiting for our stockings—'Has he come yet and is it time yet', the calls woke Mum and Dad a number of times from the early hours. The day finally arrived. We opened our stockings but were not allowed to open our other presents until after breakfast. We children were sent into the front room as soon as the fire was blazing and the room warm.

At first we just waited for the adults. We waited and waited but then heard a funny noise. 'Look' someone shouted. The door was closed but hanging behind it was a huge stocking. On top the three dolls were 'bursting out' and the stocking was moving mysteriously up the door. We rushed to the door and the adults opened it, laughing at our reactions. The dolls had labels. The big blonde doll had my name on it. Surprisingly each of us got the doll we wanted. I always wondered how they knew which to give us; later I realised they had set a trap and probably followed us upstairs. These were not second hand dolls, times were easier in 1944, and for the first time they were new. Mine had blonde curly hair, rosy cheeks and wonder of wonders, blue eyes that opened and closed. She even had lashes and she was perfect.

We played with our dolls all morning. After a while, one of my sisters walked past with a kettle of cold water to fill her doll's bath. Somehow, she poked out the eyes of my doll, with the spout of the kettle. Her eyes disappeared inside leaving gaping holes. My beautiful doll with blue eyes that opened and closed was blind, I was heartbroken and started to cry. The adults came to see what all the fuss was about.

'I'll take her to the doll's hospital and get her mended,' Aunty Kath promised.'

'Where's the hospital—when will you take her?'

'Soon, but play with her today.' I played with my blind doll all day and kept peering into her empty eyes to see where they were. I left her behind when we went home. I was so upset, I had waited and waited and asked and asked for a doll with eyes that opened and closed.

I kept asking about the doll, but the weeks went into months and she was always 'still in hospital.' The months became years and eventually I forgot about the her. Many years later when I was seventeen, I found her in a cupboard at my Aunt's house—still blind. I never dared ask why she hadn't had her repaired and I did think I might as well have had a blind doll than no doll at all. Perhaps the doll was not repairable.

Something else I wanted for years was a John Bull printing outfit. I kept asking and finally one year—there it was. Now I was going to produce a newspaper and circulate it to the family. I made a start that very day. I found the little rubber letters, that were back to front, difficult to understand. Each one had to be put in reverse order and pressed into a little wooden holder. Only when a two or three words were in place could they then be pressed into the ink. It took me all day to do a few words. I decided newspapers were out. For someone who needed to do something *yesterday*, it was very tedious. I decided I wasn't going to be a printer. When I look at the presents we wanted, they seem so very unsophisticated compared with presents for today's children. But that was how it was.

We made our own entertainment at Christmas. We played games and listened and laughed together to the comedy shows of the day. 'Itma', with Tommy Handley and Mrs Mopp, was primitive humour by today's standard; but always brought a laugh to the adults in the serious days of war. His catch phrase 'Ta ta for now,' came into everyday use along with 'Mona Lott's It's being so cheerful as keeps me going.'

One year, Mum said, 'We're going to the Pantomime, Aunty Kath's got tickets,'

'Which one, which one?' we were excited, 'is it Cinderella?'

'Jack and the Beanstalk, but you will love it,' Dad was excited—For us and for himself.

'When?'

'After Christmas, we're going to Aston Hippodrome.'

It was so exciting. The beanstalk that got bigger and bigger, how did they do that? We loved the amazing pantomime stage sets and the pretty costumes.

'Oh yes I will.'

'Oh no you won't.' we shouted.

'Oh, yes I will.'

We joined in with the banter and the shouting, which never changes, however many years pass. It was important in the dreary days of war for theatres and cinemas to stay open.

After 1944, the adults somehow managed to get food for amazing Christmas meals. I remember the dining room table at Aunt Kath's loaded with food. We had turkey and all the trimmings, mince pies and Christmas pudding aflame with brandy. Normal fare for today but in wartime difficult to acquire. After dinner came absolute silence for the King's speech and then the men washed up. Dad, by tradition, grumbled, good humouredly, that every piece of crockery and cutlery in the house had been used. Meanwhile, we children were absorbed with our books or toys and with a large box of chocolates for a special treat. I have no idea how it was acquired on ration; but there was one every year. In the increasing darkness of the winter afternoon, the adults chatted in the cosy firelight, and from time to time laughter punctuated the air. Soon they dozed off to sleep by the warm fire, the embers glowed and settled in the grate.

Eventually in the dusk, just before the curtains were drawn, the table was quietly laid for supper and gradually the house came to life again. To this day, I love those quiet times when Christmas excitement begins to bubble up again. Plates of cold turkey, ham and tongue were placed on the dining room table. Pickles and salads were added, plates of bread and butter and gradually the smell of food drifted through to where we children were playing. I remember one year standing at the dining room door and looking at all the food. In 1944 it was still wartime and I had never seen anything like it. A huge trifle laced with sherry and topped with cream was carried through. There were all sorts of cakes and of course Mum's special Christmas cake and at each plate a Christmas Cracker.

I don't think we used the black market or expected special favours in return for money in everyday life but Aunty Kath had managed to get a Turkey that Christmas. I remember overhearing about a mysterious trip by car into the middle of Wales—until it was seen that I was listening and there was silence. It was very 'hush hush' but I think that was all—although

I wonder where they got the cream for the Christmas trifle.

I was always asked what I wanted to eat. It was always a cheese sandwich. During the war, cheese was rationed and was a treat. Aunty Kath always said the same, 'Only a cheese sandwich?' That was all I wanted, that was my treat.

So in spite of shortages, Christmas was happy. When I was six, Ann and I were in the garden talking about Christmas.

'How long is it to Christmas,' said Ann.

'It's June now–so that's–one–two–I think six months.' We started to cry.

Mum came out, 'What on earth is the matter? she asked.

'It's only June and there's another six months to Christmas.' We continued crying. Christmas even with shortages was still special.

16

HOSPITALS AND HOLIDAYS

In December 1942, Ann went into hospital with a severe ear infection. She had terrible earache for several weeks and Dad put drops in and a warm bandage around her head. She had an infected mastoid bone behind her ear and was in hospital for several weeks. This was before the first antibiotics and an operation to cut out the infected bone was the only way to deal with it. In those days, children who were admitted to hospital were not allowed visitors in case they got upset. Mum wrote to her friend of how much she misses her, and how she went to look at her through a window but couldn't touch her.

The following month in January 1943, Mum herself went into hospital and was away for ten days. I learned as an adult that she had radium treatment for suspected cancer. When we saw her again she looked pale and tired. Radium treatment in those early days was vicious. Nobody told us that she was going to hospital—she just wasn't there. Today's children would 'rehearse' the situation but yesterday's children were kept in the dark.

Around the same time, I had my tonsils out. I had no idea what was going to happen to me, no-one explained. I was taken to Selly Oak Hospital and sat with Mum in a crowded room of mothers and children. I knew I was having my tonsils out but didn't know what that entailed. One by one the children disappeared until it was my turn.

'Mrs Johnson.' The doctor called us in. 'Hello Muriel, so you're having your tonsils out.' He talked to Mum and she gave me a hug and said,

' Go with the doctor.'

'Good girl,' he said and lifted me, still not understanding, onto a table. I remember a cloth made of layers of green gauze was put over my nose, it smelled funny, I guess it was chloroform. I could see lots of dots of light through the gauze—then I remember no more.

When I woke I was in a cot in a dark ward with a lot of cots with other children; my throat was very, very sore. Mum was nowhere in sight. I slept again and woke the next morning and sat up. A nurse came over and told me off for dribbling blood all over the sheet, she was very angry it seemed. She said I should have used the bowl by my head. I just stared at her, crying was too painful and I didn't know about the blood or the bowl. It was still dark and I sat looking through the bars of the cot not knowing what had happened.

One by one the children disappeared as their mothers collected them. Finally, my mother arrived. She was the very last and I thought she had left me there; I realise now she travelled a long way to collect me. My throat was sore but now I did cry. What relief to see her. She dressed me and then took me shopping for the day's food. I didn't want to walk round shops, I felt too unwell. But having tonsils out was just an overnight stop; hundreds were done every week when it was fashionable. I realise now what a dangerous operation it can be and that bleeding is a real cause for concern.

In 1943 we went on holiday. Travel must have got easier in 1941, after the raids stopped. The first week of August, was the traditional week when workers across the country took their one-week holiday. In 1938, the 'Holidays with Pay Act' had been passed. This meant that employers must make provision for holidays with pay for their workers. Offices and factories closed down everywhere as folk went away, or stayed at home and went on day trips. It became known as 'works-week.' Just one week a year!

We often went to stay for weekends, or for the holidays to Mum's friends or Dad's cousins in Talke Pits. But this year, we went to Blackpool although it was still wartime. I was six and it was the first time I had seen the sea, or could remember seeing it. We stayed in a traditional boarding house, this meant we had to be out all day after breakfast until the evening meal. Landladies were known for their strict rules about not letting guests back in during the day. It rained a lot and I remember Mum wanting to go back, but feeling she couldn't. We didn't have a car to go for a drive, or to sit in.

I don't know what we did in the rain for that wet week but there was one major excitement. 'There is a whale on the beach,' our landlady told us one morning. 'You must go and see it.'

'We certainly will,' said Dad. It was a cold drizzly morning but we hurried to the beach. There had been a fierce storm during the night and for some reason the whale had been driven onto the sands near the Pier. And then we saw it.

'It's huge,' Mum said and it smells.'

'It's dead.' Dad said, 'I wonder what happened.'

There were lots of people wandering around it and holiday makers, with Brownie cameras, taking photos. It was the first time I realised just how big whales were, it was like a huge grey mountain and smelled very fishy.

That was the holiday we first had the thrill of eating sticky pink candy-floss, it stuck to our teeth and melted into nothing. And then there was the surprise of Blackpool Rock with the name written all the way through. How did it get there?

Although it was cold Dad bought us buckets and spades. We put on our bathing suits and learned what fun it was to make sandcastles and paddle in the sea. The sea seemed a long way out and icy cold but we didn't mind. Mum and Dad sat on the beach on stripey deckchairs which had striped hoods to shade from the sun—if it came out. Dad read his newspaper and then took off his shoes, and the socks that were held up by garters and suspenders. He rolled up his trouser legs and paddled in the sea. He was a traditional British holiday maker. Men wore suits on the beach in those days and tied four knots in the corners of a handkerchief to make a sun hat, and unbelievably, women wore stockings and shoes.

We went to the hall of mirrors, a passage lined with curved and distorted mirrors. We shrieked with laughter at our changing shapes. 'Come and look at me' we shouted in turn. Mum and Dad looked on with amusement, enjoying our reactions

'Wow, look how fat I am, look at my face.' I blew my cheeks in and out like a frog.

'And I've gone thin, how does that happen?'

'Mum, Dad, can I have a penny for that machine?' I wanted to see what the Butler saw. 'Mum what *did* the butler see?'

I wanted a penny so that I could look into one of the 'pretend' telescopes to find out; but they just laughed so I never did find out! Donkeys trailed up and down the beach and of course we had a donkey ride. We sat on the sand and watched Punch and Judy. Punch, with his big stick and big nose and funny squeaky voice, whacked everyone. We shouted at Punch as he beat his wife. We watched as he threw the baby and sausages over the side of the bright stripey stand—why is everything 'seaside' stripey? We clapped as Judy got her own back and we cheered the policeman. We were as 'pleased as punch' whatever that means.

And all the time in the background, the laughing sailor rolled around and laughed – 'Ho ho ho –ha ha ha –he he he.'

17

HOLLYHOCKS AND HANDSTANDS

We finally moved further out of the City sometime in the Summer of 1944. It was still wartime and housing remained difficult to find because thousands of homes that had been destroyed. So for us, our new home was still a temporary stop and we were on the move again within four years. I was six and I had lived in four different places.

Mum still wanted to buy her own home but Dad by now was less keen. Apart from this, the money they had saved for the deposit for the house in Cherry Orchard had gone during the hard times of the war. Dad was also an ardent Labour Party supporter. After the years of poverty that affected his family since his Father died, he wanted a fairer society. To him everything should be nationalised; not just railways, mines and utilities but housing and medical care. Mum however, was different; but then she hadn't experienced the same financial hardships and difficulties as Dad.

Although Mum wasn't settled, we girls all loved the new house in Yardley Wood. It was near to a Common and was spacious and very light with a lovely big garden at the back and another at the front. There was a gravel drive down the side where hollyhocks grew in profusion along the wall. Hundreds in every colour possible, pink, purple, yellow white and mixtures of each, they grew eight-foot tall in the summer. It was a long drive and the colours were intense. making a border that everyone stopped to look at. They also were a bee trap, humming and buzzing with a myriad bees. Sometimes we closed the petals around a bee; and chased each other around the garden. Mary always shrieked the loudest, perhaps because of having the bee sting when she was evacuated.

In that front garden we learned to do cartwheels in the summer and practised handstands.

Dad said, 'All I ever see these days are upside down girls with legs in the air.'

Summer officially arrived when we were allowed to put on summer dresses. But we wanted summer dresses in the Easter holidays.

'Can we put a dress on?' Handstands were so much easier in dresses.

Mum said, 'Never cast a clout, until May is out.' But sometimes she did say, 'All right then, put them on, it's warm enough.'

One summer I was desperate to have a pair of 'open-toed' strap sandals. I asked again and again. I had seen some pretty green ones when I was shopping with Mum, I really, really wanted them.

Mum just said 'We'll see.'

Finally, we went shopping for new sandals and I had to have a pair of white ones for best. They were leather and cleaned with a white powder mixed with water and applied.

I think I whinged, until Dad said, 'I know, I'll cut the toes out of last year's sandals.' He did, at last I had my open toes, they weren't green and didn't have straps, but I was satisfied.

In the winter when the hollyhocks had gone, the wall on the drive was ideal for the ball game of 'fivers', the ball had to hit the wall in five different ways consecutively. Under the leg, over the leg, round the back, over the head, the ball bounced against the wall until we were experts. When we tired of that, the pavement outside was perfect for hours of hopscotch. I was fascinated the first time I saw hopscotch and watched older girls balancing precariously on one leg. What a compulsive game.

We skipped in season. Sometimes two people turned the rope, and we all ran through, or skipped all together singing skipping rhymes. 'All in together girls, never mind the weather girls.' We played hide and seek and off ground touch, chasing and catching each other as children have done for years. An added bonus was an enormously wide strip of grass opposite the house, perfect for games of every sort and a meeting place for all the children.

In season Mum made rhubarb pie and sometimes saved us a stick of rhubarb. Sweets were still on ration but rhubarb dipped in sugar made a delicious substitute. We dipped and sucked, dipped and sucked and grimaced at the sharp, tart taste.

Our move to this house was the beginning of a carefree childhood. The roads were almost traffic free apart from horses, clip-clopping along, delivering milk and bread. Child predators were unheard of. There were long summer days outdoors when, because of double summer time, it was light for a long after our bedtime. Nevertheless, the blackout was still rigorously in place every night when it got dark, although raids were rare by now.

One day just after we moved, I was picking raspberries in the hedge in the back garden and became aware that I was being watched. A girl of my age and height was looking at me across the gardens. I pretended to pick more raspberries. She was there the next day.

I don't know who spoke first but I said 'We've got raspberries,' with a sweep of my hand.

'So have we,' she said. It seemed to create a 'raspberry bond' between us. We became best friends. We went to school together, played together and went to Sunday School together.

Our back garden was big with lawns and borders, a garden frame for Dad's plants and long paths for us to ride our tricycle on. We all shared the 'trike.' It had three big wheels, the size of pram wheels, a basket and a saddle bag and a real brake. Most of all we loved the big green swing that Dad built. It was so very tall and the ropes so long that we could swing higher and higher until we could look out over all the other gardens. One trick was to swing as high as possible and then jump off.

Mum and Dad both enjoyed gardening in their different ways. Mum loved night scented stock and old fashioned mignonette which she planted near the back door so that the perfume wafted on the evening air. She said it reminded her of her mother. She loved all the old fashioned cottage garden flowers in the summer but in the winter she especially loved anemones with their bright jewel colours and freesia. Dad just loved being out in the garden. He built a greenhouse and grew what he called 'real English tomatoes.' They tasted wonderful. He grew cucumbers in cold frames and they tasted delicious. Sometimes, Mum sliced cucumber very thinly and marinated it in vinegar with finely sliced spring onion and a little sugar. It was left for an hour before using for sandwiches and we all loved it. Food was still rationed so Mum was always looking for ways to make it interesting.

Dad's cold frame had a wood surround and glass panels on top. One day I found a steel razor blade which he had been using to make plant cuttings. It was on a ledge inside the frame, I picked it up and started to slice fine strips of wood off the edge of the frame. It was very sharp and very satisfying when the wood came off in long strips. *Then I saw it.*

A vivid emerald green caterpillar, came looping its way along the frame. Up in an arch went one end, and then the other end drawn to follow. Without a thought I sliced the caterpillar in half. Then I felt sick. Then I felt frightened. Then I remembered my friend told me. 'If you kill someone, God will kill you.'

That green caterpillar was a *someone.* I waited to drop dead and thought of the poem we learned at school, '*Hurt no living thing, Ladybird, nor butterfly, Nor moth with dusty wing, Nor dancing gnat, nor beetle fat, Nor harmless worms that creep.' Christina Rosetti.*

Nothing happened to me, but for days I felt the 'Sword of Damocles' was hanging over my head. I learned a lesson that day about thoughtless actions, although I have probably trodden on many insects since.

Dad built a hen-run and a hen house in the garden. At last we had several hens of our own which was important in wartime. I had a special one, called Henrietta, after one of Aunty Kath's hens. I used to go and sit in the hen house and talk to her. It was a small space, smelling of sawdust and hens. The hens squawked and clucked at my intrusion, feathers and dust flying everywhere. Mum cooked special food for the chickens. Every day she heated up some chicken meal that smelled very strange. It was carried in a bucket to the hen run and scattered warm to the clucking brown hens. They enjoyed it enormously and rewarded us with eggs.

The day came when Henrietta was sacrificed. Chickens in those days were bought with their feathers on. They hung upside down from their feet on the butcher's hooks and I had seen Mum pluck the feathers many times. It seemed a huge fuss with hard to remove feathers being tugged out. I hated watching. She was a country girl and had done it many times and would laugh and say it's nothing and you'll enjoy it when it's cooked.

Mum had told me what would happen but I was only seven and didn't understand. I watched as Dad and Uncle chased and caught her and then cut off her head … the normal way in those days. She carried on running for a bit and then dropped. I felt sick and refused to eat meat from that day and became a vegetarian until I was nineteen. I couldn't believe anyone could kill Henrietta, pull out her feathers and eat her served up with vegetables and gravy.

One day, Ann and I quarrelled after she took the pram I was playing with.

'Give it back.'

'No,' she pulled it away from me.

I tried to pull it back. 'I was playing with it first.'

'No, I want it, we've got to share.'

I couldn't get it back, so I hit her on the head with my doll. She screamed and ran to Mum. I ran to the hen house and waited. I waited and waited. All through the afternoon I waited. The hens clucked and squawked and scraped the dust and made me sneeze. It seemed I waited for hours in the hen house, I was so scared. Eventually Ann fetched me for tea.

'Mum says you have been punished enough.'

To my relief, she was still alive but with a bruise and being cosseted. She told me, as an adult, that she remembers coming to fetch me with a 'smug' look on her face—her words. There was no mention of her punishment.

The hen run had very high wire netting fences. One night, a fox dug under the fence and killed all the hens. Dad complained bitterly that it killed not one hen but all of them. He said he would not have more hens after that. In retrospect, I realise that the outlay for the hens was probably considerable.

The Yardley Wood house seemed very spacious and light. The back room was used as our sitting room, as it overlooked the garden. The house had electricity but also gas lighting which was fascinating. Although we didn't use it, Dad could turn on the gas and light the mantles with a match. The lights hissed and burned in strange colours. Gas lighting continued in some Birmingham houses until the 1970s.

In the back room was a settee and chairs covered in pale green loose covers. One night, Mary screamed uncontrollably. She screamed and screamed and then jumped onto the settee and pulled her legs up and was quite hysterical. Eventually we learned she had seen a mouse run under the loose cover of the settee.

When Mary screamed she really did scream! We learned just how loud when Ann and I decided to play a trick on her after bedtime and blackout.

'I know, let's get under Mary's bed and scare her.' We crawled in the dark along the landing to her room.

'Shh, don't make a sound,'—'Don't let her hear.'

We quietly crawled under her bed. The bed was two foot six inches off the floor, with a mesh spring base.

'Boo,' louder, 'Boo, ooo.' with that we humped our backs up under the bed; poor Mary was catapulted into the air.

She screamed, 'Dad, help, Dad'. What a terrible shock in the dark, for someone who was already very nervous. Help came quickly and we were told off.

The table with the iron mark from Church Road, stood in the middle of the back room. Underneath were ledges on which we children hid toys. It was the perfect hiding place. It was definitely invented by us and no other child had *ever* thought of hiding under the table during meal times. At least I thought that, until without prompting, my own children did the same. I have a tea time memory of Mum and Dad pretending not to notice we were taking food from the table and giggling as we ate our picnic underneath.

'Where are the girls?' asked Dad.

'I don't know but they are missing their tea.' Mum played along perfectly.

'Who took that sandwich?' complained Dad. 'I was just about to eat it.' Giggles under the table.

Every now and then, a hand mysteriously appeared holding a plate with food. Once we tied Dad's shoe laces to the table leg and he pretended he didn't know, making loud exclamations as he discovered he was immobilised.

The same table figures in another experience of those days. We went to see the Wizard of Oz and just loved it. When our cousins came to stay we played make believe games about the Wizard. We knew the songs by heart.

We chanted 'Follow the yellow brick road,' chasing each other around the table again and again. The impetus increased as we changed to 'Lions and tigers and bears—oh my, lions and tigers and bears—oh my.'

Faster and faster we ran after each other until I tripped and fell. I put my hand out to stop myself—right onto the red hot coals of the blazing fire.

The game stopped. I can't remember what happened but it was really painful and difficult to sleep that night and for several nights. I think Mum put butter on—a regular treatment in those days for burns. No idea then of plunging it into cold water to disperse the heat. Dad dressed my hand every day. He was gentle with wounds and was always the one who took out splinters. He had learned First Aid as an Air Raid Warden. He taught us how to put on bandages and slings. Sometimes if we had an infected wound, he made a bread poultice and applied it steaming hot, to draw out the infection. Those were days before antibiotics. Eventually my hand healed without scars but I didn't visit a Doctor.

In the days before the start of the NHS, medical care had to be paid for. Dad was covered by the National Insurance Act of 1911 which provided free health care and medicine for all wage earners between sixteen and seventy. The scheme was compulsory and those who were employed each paid 4d a week from their wages, the employer added 3d and the state 2d. Workers were guaranteed unemployment benefit for seven weeks in a year. A person off sick and getting treatment was 'On the Panel.'

However, that 9d a week didn't cover wives and children and I don't know how Mum and Dad made provision for the rest of the family. Before the war they paid into Birmingham Ideal Benefit Society for health insurance. I had my tonsils out, Ann had her mastoid operation and Mum had radium treatment. They had to pay for all of these and in one of Mum's letters to her friend, she commented that her consultation with the gynaecologist had cost £2.2s.

Nationally the general health of the population was poor because of the inability of many to pay for the simplest of medicines. However, plans were in hand to change this even during wartime. The Beveridge Report of 1942, recommended compulsory insurance contributions to cover free health care for *every* person. That included unemployment benefit, sickness, maternity benefit, widows and old age benefits. The Act was passed in 1946 but didn't come into effect until 1948. Also in 1945, the Family Allowance Act provided for a regular sum for second and subsequent children to be paid to the mother. These were momentous steps that would radically change society.

Another winter passed and the grim war continued. The United States did not initially get involved in WW11, as it was seen as a European conflict, although they did provide financial assistance and equipment to Britain. In December 1941, the Japanese raided Pearl Harbour and destroyed a large part of the US navy and a few days later Hitler declared war on the United States. The US then officially entered the war. American troops started arriving in England during 1942-3 and set up camps across the country and some were billeted on part of the Common. I remember the Common standing waist high in corn because all available land was farmed for food.

The Americans brought with them the wonderful music of Glen Miller and of course silk stockings, chewing gum and chocolate. Those were the days of the afternoon 'Tea Dance' and dancing to the music of the day on 'wind up' gramophone records. We didn't know much about that as children but I will never forget hearing 'Lili Marlene', the most hauntingly beautiful song of WW11. Even as a child it caught my attention. Written by a German composer, it was a hit for both German and Allied Forces. Marlene Dietrich, with her mysterious husky voice, began to sing it in 1943.

'Underneath the lantern by the barrack gate, Darling I remember the way you used to wait, T'was there that you whispered tenderly, That you loved me, You'd always be, My Lili of the lamplight, My own Lili Marlene.'

Soon Vera Lynn, the 'Forces Sweetheart,' was singing it to Servicemen all over the world. Just as popular were her songs, 'We'll meet again' and 'There'll be Bluebirds over the White Cliffs of Dover.'

The Yanks sometimes came to buy fish and chips at the shop on the corner and we stared with curiosity at their different uniforms and friendly ways. Some of the kids really did say, 'Got any gum chum,' but I don't know if they got any! Sometimes, from that chip shop, we bought a pennyworth of chips with 'bits' from the fish batter. It was smothered in salt and vinegar and wrapped up in newspaper.

Not very hygienic but delicious—but where had the newspapers been? *Who or what had been sitting on them*? Perhaps it's not a good idea to think too much about the state of the newspapers!

18

A NEW SCHOOL 1944

It was the middle of the summer term in 1944 when I started at Trittiford Road Primary School On my first day I sat at the back and didn't know anyone. I didn't want to be there and missed my old friends, the teacher didn't even speak to me or welcome me. On the same day, another pupil who had been away for six months in a sanatorium came back. The teacher welcomed her and told us all about TB and how she had been to an 'Open Air School,' and told us to be friends with her. I didn't fancy being away from home for six months.

I put up my hand, 'Please Miss can I go to the toilet.'

'Yes, but be quick.'

I ran across the playground to the rank of outside toilets and suddenly thought of Mum and felt very homesick. I walked out of the gates and ran home. My mother was washing, so it was a Monday.

She looked up, 'What are you doing here?'

'I just wanted to see you.'

She picked me up and cuddled me, 'I'll give you something to eat before you go back.'

'I don't want to go back.'

'You have to go back, the Attendance Officers will come and I will go to prison if I keep you at home.'

The thought of Mum going to prison was worse than going to open air school. Everything is 'black and white' in a child's mind. I remember it was the usual Monday wash-day lunch, chips and cold meat. I went back for afternoon school and no-one asked where I had been. Perhaps the bell had gone, anyway, I wasn't missed. So different from today's high level security.

My new teacher's name was Miss Buggins and Mum used to laugh and wonder if she was related to Grandma Buggins. During the war, there was a radio programme with Grandma Buggins giving advice and helpful wartime hints to housewives. I don't know whether she was related, although it is an unusual name.

In her class we sat in rows of desks, moving up or down depending on good or bad marks. There were dinner monitors to collect dinner tickets and chalk monitors to clean the blackboard. We had milk monitors to give out the milk and ink monitors to fill the inkwells. Inkwells were little porcelain containers sunk into the top corner of each desk. The ink came in big heavy glass bottles that had to be tipped carefully to fill the inkwell. Sheets of blotting paper were handed out by the blotting paper monitor.

In time we learned to take on responsibility. In fact, when she said, 'Who can tell the time?'

I waved my hand frantically, 'I can.'

'Go to the hall and check the time on the clock.' There was a big school clock in the hall, and I stood there looking at it for a long time trying to work out what the hands were saying. I just wasn't sure—actually I had no idea. I was only just seven, not many children had watches and there was only one clock in our house. Even our teacher didn't have a watch.

Eventually a teacher came by. 'What are you doing here?'

'I've come to see the time. . .but I can't tell it.' She told me the time and I skipped back to class.

We learned from the blackboard on an easel at the front. We stood up and recited and learned the 'times tables' together in unison.

'One times two is two—two times two is four—three times two is six.'

We had spelling lessons when we spelled aloud, again in unison 'C-a-t spells cat.'

We recited lots and lots of poetry together. Somehow that method of teaching did work and a love of poetry, has never left me. We were slapped on the hand with a ruler from time to time but it didn't harm our 'psyche' and discipline was good. Mum prided herself that she left the teachers to get on with their work and wasn't continually up at the school, 'As some are.' — so she said.

We had a weekly walk to Trittiford Park and nature lessons on the spot.

We collected flowers and leaves and nuts in season. We grew bulbs in water and beans in jam jars lined with blotting paper; we watched and waited as the roots and the sprouts grew up and down the side of the jar. We learned about trees and birds and animals and flowers and drew and wrote about them in our little books. Nature lessons were really important in that school. Not much different from school today perhaps, but I gained a love for nature and the seasons that was to last. I always loved the autumn and one year at school we learned a poem by Keats:

'Season of mists and mellow fruitfulness, Close bosom friend of the maturing sun, Conspiring with him how to bless with fruit, the vines that round the thatch eaves run. To bend with apples the moss'd cottage-trees, And fill all fruit with ripeness to the core;'

How clever I thought, to express the autumn so perfectly. Well—I didn't think those actual words but that's what I meant. I could just see and feel the autumn through the words.

I have my school exercise books from those days. One of them records a day when I was seven and we walked in a 'crocodile' from school to Trittiford Park. It was Autumn 1944.

I wrote, 'I collected beech nuts and made a dear little basket and saw a swan on the lake.'—so much for my own efforts at recording the autumn.

A lady came to the school gates in the Autumn. She sold toffee apples from a big old black pram. She picked the apples from her garden and then dunked them into a delicious toffee. The toffee covered the apples perfectly and ran down to form a platform of toffee that held the apples with their sticks vertically. When she had sold them all, she had a reserve store under the removable bottom of the pram. We used to beg Mum for a penny to buy one and were occasionally rewarded. People were very resourceful in the war in all sorts of ways.

Another exercise book I have, is dated May 1945 when I was just eight. Paper and books were short in wartime and our exercise books were handmade by the teacher and stitched together. One day I wrote about Tinker, our cat from Bayswater Road. It was writing practice, using the old fashioned type of pen with a steel nib, dipped into ink.

I laboriously wrote, 'My pet is a kitten, it is black and white and its name is Tinker. It sometimes sits on my shoulder and goes to sleep. Our kitten used to be our neighbour's cat but they sold it to us. The kitten liked to play with balls and string.'

We didn't buy the cat from the neighbour; I think I just wanted to use the word 'neighbour.' It was hard work writing with a pen and ink; punctuation and spelling was the last thing on my mind. The inkwells in the desks were always stuffed with blotting paper by the boys. At least I think—or am sure, it was the boys. The blotting paper came out in a big lump on the nib and suddenly blots appeared from nowhere. That meant a red circle around the blot and a comment. Exercise books with my writing in pencil, show I had mastered the art of writing, it was just pen and ink that caused the problems.

My book is filled with the sort of writing unheard of today. We had writing practice every day, and one day we copied a proverb, 'Go to the ant thou sluggard and learn from her ways and be wise.' Afterwards we learned what that meant and were taught a lesson about hard work! Another one was, 'A boy makes no noise when he smiles, a boy makes very little noise when he sighs, a boy makes much noise when he screeches.'

There are lots of poems in that book, creative writing, spelling practice and a lot of Scripture written with my pen—the nib dipped into ink. Scripture lessons were important and all schools had daily assemblies and started with prayer. I remember the Head Master telling us Bible stories and drawing life-lessons from them.

Another day, I wrote that Mum and Dad had taken us to the Botanical Gardens in the Easter holidays. We loved the hot houses and the fountains and the monkey houses.

'Look at the monkeys.' We stopped and looked and called to them.

'Don't touch them,' said Mum when they reached tiny hands through the cages, 'They are very strong.'

We stopped at the parrot cages trying to get the cockatoos to talk. They just squawked and climbed the wires, gripping with beaks and black clawed feet. But my lasting memory is of the gardens, and of the intense perfume that filled the air from wallflowers that massed the borders in springtime. It was quite incredible, and the smell of wallflowers today immediately calls to mind the sunshine and the perfume of those borders.

We had Christmas parties at school in spite of the war. The classrooms were decorated with colourful paper chains that we made; one year we made pretty Chinese lanterns and hung them on string across the classroom. We took jelly and cakes to school on the last day of term and played party games during the afternoon.

One teacher told us very firmly, 'If you go door to door carol singing in the holidays, you must knock first, then ask politely if you can sing a carol.' We listened intently as she said, 'You represent the school and you must always be polite!' and she continued, 'I will hear about any of you being rude.'

I was eight; and the war just over, when the school put on a performance of the 'Bluebird', by Maurice Maeterlinck. It is a Christmas fairy story about a little girl and her brother who search for a bluebird that will bring them happiness. In the story the utensils in their cottage home come to life and become animated characters — wood, water, fire, bread, light, milk etc. I don't know why I wasn't cast as a lead character — or the fairy godmother or even one of the 12 dancing hours, but I was grateful to be water.

'Can you act water and sound like water?' said Miss Buggins. *I certainly could.* I 'whoooooooshed' and wailed and possibly screamed and she said, 'Good that's it'.

I was draped in a sheet of blue polythene — all the teachers were fascinated by this new product — and I wailed across the stage making the loudest noise I could. No one complained but why I thought I sounded like water I don't **know.**

It was a good school and I had a good educational foundation for the years ahead. Miss Wood, my class teacher in my last year, was very significant to me. She was tall and thin with brown hair and beady eyes. She was very, very strict but fair. She was meticulous and thorough in her teaching and pronunciation of grammar. She taught us diction and correct pronunciation and we had elocution lessons every week on Friday. I remember standing in our rows of desks and repeating 'How now brown cow.' That phrase was used to teach 'rounded' vowel sounds—whatever they were. She was quick to correct when we got it wrong. Mum was also quick to correct what she thought was bad grammar.

Miss Wood loved poetry and we learned poems for the seasons as they arrived, or for special events. In November we learned about poppies and Remembrance Day and the famous First World War poem. 'In Flanders fields the poppies blow, between the crosses, row on row, that mark our place; and in the sky, the larks, still bravely singing, fly scarce heard amid the guns below.'

She read the story of Hiawatha in a voice and rhythm that captured our interest so that we wanted to hear more. . .'By the shore of Gitche Gumee, By the shining Big-Sea-Water'. . .I always remember how she held our attention as she recited the verses.

She coached us rigorously for the 11 plus exam that all eleven-year-olds had to take in their last year in primary school. The Education Act, which became Law in 1946, aimed to provide free education for every child up to the age of at least fifteen years. The 11 plus was a means of allocating each child to the school best suited to his or her abilities. In the end it turned out to be an unfair system and it was changed in the 1960s for a fairer system of Comprehensive Education. However, for twenty years or so, the 11 plus reigned supreme as the means of selection.

Dad was really keen that we should have the education he missed out on. I took the exam and passed for Grammar School in 1948, in my last year at Trittiford Road School. To me it was just an exam which seemed to cause anxiety to Mum and Dad and had some strange questions which didn't make sense. I did enjoy the creative writing question, so perhaps that was where I gained marks. From a selfish point of view, although an unfair system, I am grateful I had the opportunity to go to Kings Norton Grammar School.

The present Trittiford Road School website has a *report of the school from 1950* which refers to, 'The excellent standards of work in English and Arithmetic as well as reading aloud, RE, music and physical instruction, especially country dancing both English and Scandinavian types,' ... 'it is clear for a very long time that the standards set and the resulting achievement have been high in what has been attempted. The ethos of the school is splendid.'

I would whole heartedly endorse all of this.

19

D–DAY 1944

After the blitz on England, from 1941 Hitler concentrated on Europe where many countries were under Nazi occupation. Russia became involved, Africa and also Japan and the Pacific. It really was a 'World-wide War.' At a meeting to work out priorities, the US President Franklin Roosevelt and Winston Churchill agreed that Germany must be defeated first and then Japan, then Burma and the occupied countries of the Pacific.

Meanwhile preparations began for the Allied D-Day landings in France in 1944. Allied troops included British, American and Canadian. Secret plans were made for a massive invasion to liberate Europe, starting with landings in Normandy. The campaign was code named, 'Operation Overlord' and over three million servicemen were involved. The weather conditions had to be right and every vessel possible had been commandeered from ports around the south coast of England. Suitable weather conditions finally arrived on 6 June, 1944.

During that day thousands of Allied troops landed on the beaches of Normandy in northern France. Simultaneously thousands of paratroops and glider-borne troops were dropped behind enemy lines. The landings were preceded by air attacks along the French coast by RAF planes and American bombers.

Reporter Cornelius Ryan wrote a superb account of the landings in his book 'The Longest Day' first published in 1959.

'They came, rank after relentless rank, ten lanes wide, twenty miles across, five thousand ships of every description. There were fast new attack transports, slow rust-

scarred freighters, small ocean liners, Channel steamers, hospital ships, weather-beaten tankers, coasters and swarms of fussing tugs. There were endless columns of shallow-draft landing ships, great wallowing vessels, some of them almost 350 feet long. Ahead of the convoys were processions of mine sweepers, Coast Guard cutters, buoy-layers and motor launches. Barrage balloons flew above the ships. Squadrons of fighter planes weaved below the clouds. And surrounding this fantastic cavalcade of ships packed with men, guns, tanks, motor vehicles and supplies were a formidable array of 702 warships.'

Utah Beach, Juno Beach, Omaha Beach,
Pegasus Bridge, Sword Beach, Arromanches.

A foothold was won in Europe. The most recent figures indicate over four thousand allied forces died in the D-Day landings. In the ensuing Battle of Normandy there were an estimated *209 thousand allied casualties.* Thousands of civilians died and nearly six hundred towns and villages were destroyed. The total number of dead was over 425 thousand Allied and German troops.

It was the beginning of the end of the war. But there was another year before complete victory as war continued around the world. *A year later, the estimated loss of life worldwide was 60 million, not including wounded.* WW11 was the deadliest military conflict ever in human history and the lessons must never be forgotten.

After the D-Day landings, there was a year of increasing shortages, although we children were sheltered from it in many ways. We were growing up in a Birmingham scarred by the raids. Many families were homeless and we always seemed to have lodgers. The Government now expected—and sometimes 'requisitioned' the spare rooms in houses for accommodation.

The city centre was almost unrecognisable to our parents, so many familiar places had gone although the Town Hall survived and a lot of Corporation Street and Victoria Square. Rebuilding did not begin until after the war. The sight of derelict bomb sites with barbed wire, was normal for many years. Life was bleak.

However, the end was near. By the spring of 1945, the Soviets were approaching the German capital of Berlin from the east, and the Western Allies were approaching from the west. Knowing defeat was imminent, on 30 April, 1945, Hitler along with his mistress Eva Braun, committed suicide in his bunker in Germany.

In the following week German troops in Italy laid down their arms, then German troops in Holland, Denmark and Germany, surrendered to Field Marshall Montgomery. Finally, on Monday 7 May, 1945, at 2:30am, General Jodl and Grand Admiral Donitz signed the unconditional surrender of all German, land, sea and air forces in Europe at the Allied headquarters in Rheims.

The news was seeping through little by little over the weekend, even though no official British announcement had been made. *Later on Monday, bell ringers nationwide were put on standby for a victory peal.* The home office issued a circular that bonfires would be allowed and gave permission that material for bunting, could be purchased *without coupons*, providing it was in red, white or blue.

20

BELLS RING ... FLAGS FLY

One morning, that same week in May 1945, I woke to the sound of loud shouting and laughter. The smell of bacon wafted upstairs. I ran almost tumbled downstairs, 'What's going on. . .what's going on?'

Mum and Dad were dancing around the room together shouting 'The wars over, the war's over. . .it's over, it's over. . .it's over. 'They danced together then threw their arms in the air whirling around the room.

Then Dad ran to the blackout curtains and dragged them down shouting 'We won't need these again.'

They were wild with excitement. They had just heard the news that Germany had unconditionally surrendered at 2:30am on Monday 7 May, 1945. Winston Churchill spoke to the nation on the wireless and the King also broadcast a message to his people. The next two days were declared National Holidays.

Church bells rang out across Britain for the first time since war started. Everywhere in Birmingham the bunting went up, Union Jacks were pulled out of storage, home-made flags and anything that would make a bright splash of colour was hung up. The fountain was lit up in town and an illuminated bus toured the neighbourhood. There were bright lights everywhere in reaction to the blackout. We had a street party on the green with singing and dancing and a massive bonfire. Victory in Europe. . .VE day, had arrived.

Flags flew. . .church bells rang again. Is it any wonder that we celebrated all day, and all night on 8 May, 1945?

On 13 May there was a Victory Parade of 16 thousand members of the armed services through the centre of Birmingham, finishing in Victoria Square, where the Lord Mayor took the salute. It took half an hour to pass by the watching crowd. One hundred thousand people lined the streets, standing shoulder to shoulder and sitting on every available window ledge. Remembrance services at the Hall of Memory were attended by thousands.

In his message to the nation, Winston Churchill speaking from the Cabinet room at Number 10 Downing Street, paid tribute to the men and women who laid down their lives for victory as well as to all those who had 'fought valiantly' on land, sea and in the air.

'We may allow ourselves a brief period of rejoicing; but let us not forget for a moment the toil and efforts that lie ahead. Japan with all her treachery and greed, remains unsubdued. We must now devote all our strength and resources to the completion of our task, both at home and abroad. *Advance Britannia.*

Over a million people gathered in London and huge crowds along the Mall outside Buckingham Palace; they cheered as the King, Queen and the two Princesses came out onto the balcony. Elizabeth and Margaret, thrilled by the crowds and the excitement, slipped out anonymously to join the fun and celebrations. Earlier tens of thousands of people had listened intently as the King's speech was relayed by loudspeaker to those who gathered in Trafalgar Square and Parliament Square.

The Royal Family had stayed in London throughout the war and was a great support and encouragement to the nation. The King and Queen made many visits to blitzed areas and in 1945 the 18-year-old Princess Elizabeth joined the Women's Auxiliary Territorial Service training as a driver of military trucks.

As liberation news arrived from the continent the nation began to understand the truth and the awful facts of what had happened under Hitler's regime. In 1942 the British Foreign Secretary, Anthony Eden, had told the House of Commons about the mass executions of Jews by Germans in occupied Europe. He described how the German authorities were carrying out Hitler's intention to exterminate the Jewish people in Europe. He told how hundreds of thousands of men, women and children were being transported from German occupied territory, to Eastern Europe in conditions of appalling horror and brutality. Those who were sick or injured were left to die of exposure or starvation or killed in mass executions.

After the war ended, the full story began to emerge as allied troops liberating concentration camps, confronted unspeakable conditions. Piles of corpses lay unburied. Surviving inmates resembled skeletons because of the lack of food, compounded by months and years of maltreatment. Many were so weak that they could hardly move.

The stories were told in films and the news in cinemas. I watched with Mum.

'It's terrible, terrible, terrible,' said Mum, 'no-one knew. . .we didn't know.'

'But why?' I asked.

'It was Hitler, he was a wicked man, he wanted to get rid of the Jews.'

'But why?'

I can't remember her answer, but remember her saying, 'We also did some dreadful things in the war.'

'What did we do.' I needed to know.

'Well for one thing, we bombed Dresden when the war was nearly over.' Mum remembered how the beautiful City of Coventry was blitzed to the ground but the British bombing of Dresden was even worse. 'There was no resistance there, it was a beautiful old City with lots of Museums.' War she explained is always terrible, whichever side.

Later, in school we were taught that many Germans knew little of Nazi hatred and obsessions. We were linked up with German school children to write and be pen-friends as peace was encouraged even at that level.

Adolf Hitler was responsible for millions of deaths in World War II but his hatred and treatment of the Jews was obsessive. He murdered two-thirds of all European Jews in his 'Final Solution', totalling six million, with five thousand Jewish communities wiped out.

As well as Jews, gypsies, communists, Poles, and underground resistance fighters were all sent to concentration camps. There were thirty-nine main camps where medical experiments, including sterilisation and castration, were carried out.

When British troops liberated Belsen concentration camp in April 1945 they found sixty thousand starving and suffering with TB, Typhus and exposure. Mass evacuation of the camp began on 21 April and many were transferred to emergency hospitals.

'A new British drug saved thousands from death by injections of protein hydrolysate. This, when injected into the veins of a starving person, revived him to such an extent that within six to twenty-four hours he was able to eat normally. From then, return to health was rapid. Deaths were reduced from two hundred a day to twenty. The drug was produced by five specialist factories turned over to producing it. The drug was flown in transport planes direct to the camps and medical centres — Edwin Tetlow, Daily Mail Special Correspondent.

It was still a few months after VE day before the Japanese finally surrendered when the US dropped two atomic bombs. On 6 August, 1945, the bomb, named 'Little Boy,' exploded two thousand feet above Hiroshima Hospital, with a force equivalent to 12 thousand tons of TNT. Fourteen thousand died as a direct result of the bombing. In the following five years, another 60 thousand died of related causes.

Hiroshima was a city of military importance. It contained the 2nd Army Headquarters, which commanded the defence of all of southern Japan and was a communications centre and an assembly area for troops.

The second bomb, called 'Fat Man,' exploded over Nagasaki, on 9 August, 1945. By the end of the year, 70 thousand people had lost their lives due to the bombing. Another 14 thousand died within the next five years. The bombs killed men, women, and children as well as military personnel. Victory in Japan, or VJ day, was on 15 August 1945.

The total carnage of WW11 on both sides was unbelievable and uncountable. It seems however sophisticated the world becomes, when dialogue and diplomacy fail, humans still resort to physical violence to subject and control those of different views.

21

ADVANCE BRITANNIA

Churchill stirred the nation to face the challenge ahead when he announced in May 1945, that the war was over. 'We must now devote all our strength and resources to the completion of our task, both at home and abroad. *Advance Britannia.*'

At home Britain finally settled down to rebuild the nation. The country was almost bankrupt and was dominated by the consequences of the war. Austerity and the rationing of many things continued until 1954. To add to the problem, bread, at 4d per loaf, which had not been rationed during the war, was rationed from 1945 for three years. Cuts were also made to both the bacon and the fat rations. There were lean years to come.

Our Britannia was Birmingham. The city looked bleak with its derelict bomb sites surrounded by barbed wire and covered in weeds. There were six thousand homeless and many more thousands with property damage because of the blitz. Extensive rebuilding, as well as new building was required. Herbert Manzoni, the City Engineer, and Architect John Madin, prior to the war, had already been planning major redevelopments of slum areas.

After the war the housing department faced three problems. Unsafe property because of bomb damage; the need to re-house the homeless because of destruction of their property; the re-housing of those who lived in unsanitary back to back housing. It was a massive task which eventually resulted in the building of new housing estates and blocks of high rise flats

In 1944, the government announced plans for the production of prefabricated buildings. Birmingham purchased and built a total of four thousand prefabs. Each had a living room, two bedrooms and a modern kitchen and bathroom and was intended to last for ten years. The majority of prefabs lasted much longer and many people loved them and would not move out when the time came for them to be demolished. Some are still standing and cherished in many parts of the country.

In the city centre there were plans for the redevelopment of the Bullring; as well as traffic management schemes which resulted in ugly concrete ring roads and tower blocks. Dozens of fine Victorian buildings were to be demolished including the old Central Library.

I loved the old Library. There was an almost tangible 'hush' and awe about it. Those magnificent rooms of learning and culture belonged to a slower and more elegant era. Beautiful high ceilings, a wide sweeping staircase and ornate decoration. But it was inevitable it would go as more space was needed than the premises could offer, and the storage facilities were inadequate. It was eventually pulled down in 1978.

After the war many people, my parents included, wanted to be rid of the old and of all reminders of the awful past. Victoriana in any form was definitely out. Victorian property was really cheap to buy and new and modern was all the rage. Mum threw out everything old, treasures included.

However, after years of drabness, Birmingham is at last being transformed into an attractive modern city. The Town Hall is no longer a traffic surrounded island. The beautiful stonework glows now that the soot and grime of centuries has been removed. As teenagers, when meeting friends there, we would say, '*See you under the arches,*' but our meeting place has now been attractively glassed in and the interior refurbished.

New Street has literally blossomed with trees, giving a feeling of life and beauty to the city. The Bullring, to me, is both a loss and a bonus but it could never be the same again. Gas Street Basin is a winner especially having arisen from its unsavoury past. The pedestrian areas, the parks and the Symphony Hall make Birmingham a city to be proud of. We often return and now I am eager to see the new library and especially New Street Station. I wonder what our war-weary parents would have thought.

Meanwhile as Britannia was advancing, much was happening around the world. It is impossible to write about it in any detail but some things were really significant. It must never happen again—The United Nations and NATO were established to make sure it didn't happen again.

The United Nations, the UN, began as a result of a secret meeting in 1941 between President Roosevelt and Winston Churchill. They met to discuss plans for a future after the war. The result was a charter that all countries should have a democratic government. All countries would engage in trade freely with one another and would share in world prosperity and all countries would seek to reduce their weaponry.

The title 'United Nations' was adopted and used by all those nations who were at war with Germany, Italy, and Japan which had formed a military alliance in September 1940.

Twenty-six nations signed the charter, the purpose of which would be to maintain international security and peace. It was also to tackle international economic, social and humanitarian problems. The number of nations participating increased and on 25 June, 1945, the representatives of 50 nations met to sign the charter in San Francisco.

NATO—The North Atlantic Treaty Organisation was created in 1949. The headquarters is in Belgium. It now has 28 members and is an intergovernmental military alliance. Member countries join together for international peacekeeping operations; they agree that if any one country is attacked, the other countries will come to help them.

When NATO admitted West Germany into membership, the Soviet Union withdrew all its satellite states in Eastern Europe into the Warsaw Pact in May 1955. This resulted in the Cold War, mainly between the USA and the USSR.

The Cold war dominated international affairs for decades and many major crises occurred; including the Cuban Missile Crisis, the Vietnam War, the Hungarian Revolution and the building of the Berlin Wall. In particular, the Suez Canal Crisis was a great concern. In July 1956, Egyptian President Nasser, supported by the Soviet, seized and nationalised the Suez Canal for Egypt.

The Canal Company was set up in 1858 and the canal was built by the French to connect the Mediterranean Sea and the Red Sea, giving access to the Far East. It is one of the world's busiest shipping lanes. Under the terms of an international convention, signed in 1888, the canal is open to vessels of all nations without discrimination, in peace and war.

When the Canal was seized, French and British forces attempted to take back the canal but were threatened by the Soviet Union if they did not withdraw. They eventually withdrew under pressure from Eisenhower who also cautioned the Soviet from getting involved.   .

22

GENERAL ELECTION—LABOUR VICTORY

A General Election was held in 1945 in the aftermath of the victory in Europe; the landslide Labour victory was a huge shock to wartime leader Winston Churchill. The Conservatives expected that because of his leadership skills through the war, he would be re-elected as Prime Minister. The Conservatives did not understand that the majority of the population wanted change from the pre-war 'social deprivations' of the 1930s. These desires had been put aside for the war effort but at the end of the war they had surfaced again.

Britannia advanced. The country both wanted and needed change. The poverty and deprivation of large numbers of the population had to be tackled. The unsanitary and crowded living conditions of millions of city dwellers were the breeding ground for disease. Slums had to be demolished and new homes built in a healthier environment. A health service was needed that would give free treatment to all people. Industrial Birmingham was in the forefront of the drive for change.

The Labour Party, led by Clement Attlee, campaigned for change and won the election with a large majority. He announced that if elected he would introduce the Welfare State outlined in the 1942 Beveridge Report. The report, drawn up during the war, included the establishment of a National Health Service with free health care for all. It included unemployment and sickness benefit, maternity benefit and widows and old age benefits. Insurance would be made compulsory for all working adults with contributions from the State, from employers and also employees. The

National Health Service Act was passed in 1946 and came into effect in July 1948. For the first time, *anywhere in the world,* there was free health care for all on the basis of need.

Aneurin Bevan, a Welsh miner who became a Labour politician, steered the Bill through the House of Commons. He said, *'In spite of our economic and financial anxieties, we are able to do the most civilised thing in the world and put the welfare of the sick before every other consideration.'*

Dad, had voted Labour and was delighted. Both his father and mother and his first children had died without adequate healthcare. It was time for change. Later, he went into the Queen Elizabeth Hospital and had a gastrectomy (stomach removed) under the new NHS and was cured of a life-long problem of repeated perforations of his stomach ulcer.

Dad was the returning Officer for the local ward and we took him sandwiches during the day and joined him in the night when he read out the results. Election fever never failed to excite us as girls and still does today —although I prefer to watch the results arrive from an easy chair and the comfort of the Television. But then I am a floating voter!

A new Education Act also came into effect in 1946. Nationalisation of the nation's industries was another election commitment of Clement Attlee. This would mean that any profit made by these industries went to the country and not to shareholders. The coal industry was nationalised in 1947. The new National Coal Board offered paid holidays, sick pay and rest homes for miners to recover after mining accidents. Safety also became an important issue. But the pay of miners did not improve and there were still strikes. Railways were nationalised in 1948 and iron and steel in 1949.

There was also a big drive to build good quality Council homes and flats and for a period of time, the government continued to restrict the building and sale of private homes. Building materials, which were in short supply, were diverted into Council schemes.

Dad was thrilled with all the changes. That was inevitable after the years of real hardship his family had gone through. It was strange that although he was in favour of general nationalisation, he wanted us girls to get the best education possible. He wanted us to pass the entrance exam for Grammar School.

The Education Act which became Law in 1946 aimed to provide free education for every child up to the age of 15 years. It was a tripartite system consisting of Grammar Schools, Technical Schools and Secondary Modern schools. The Grammar Schools were mostly the old fee paying private schools, which now became free for those who passed the entrance exam.

Every child took the 11 plus exam, so that each could be allocated to the school best suited to his or her abilities and aptitudes. In the end it turned out to be an unfair and discriminatory system. The system was changed in the 1960s for a fairer system of Comprehensive Education for every child.

But these were momentous, history making changes. The country changed from a society that favoured the rich at the beginning of the 1940s to a welfare state with equal and fairer opportunities for everyone at the end of the decade. It was also a huge task for the government, as many different areas were tackled simultaneously, in spite of shortage of money and materials.

As for the children…we were going to be given every opportunity that our parents had been denied. A new world would be at our feet.

One of the immediate effects of the new NHS was the establishing of regular school medical checks for each child, including eye and dental inspections. Problems identified, were referred for treatment to the now free health service. In the drive to improve dental care, I remember all children were given free round tins of Gibbs Dentifrice toothpaste and toothbrushes. Children also started to wear braces to correct their teeth if needed. What has become a fashion today was unusual then.

Adults also qualified for free dental treatment and many who had previously treated themselves with home remedies, now registered with Dentists. I well remember the stories told about pulling out teeth—tying a loose tooth with a thread to a door handle; then slamming the door. Those days were gone. The days had come of slow drills, whining away for ages, and no anaesthetic injections. Gas was widely used for extractions.

The result seems to have created a fashion for dentures. Perhaps, because of previous poor treatment or years of neglect, many people had all their teeth extracted and dentures fitted. I remember Dad had his teeth out and I came home from school to find him with a bowl spitting blood and no teeth. It was a shock. It seemed very drastic, especially as I can't remember him having tooth problems. Later he was the proud new owner of a set of false teeth.

In the coming years when I was nursing at Dudley Road Hospital, it was normal for older patients to have dentures and containers were placed for them on the bedside lockers. Many a set was lost in a patient's bed, or patients helped themselves to the wrong sets from lockers! These were the years when older people with dentures, grimaced and gyrated the dentures around in their mouths as they tried to get rid of crumbs from under the plate. Teeth appeared in the most extraordinary positions and it was a source for comedian's jokes.

There was also a run it seems on eye tests and free spectacles. It is reported that *the two million pounds* set aside to pay for free spectacles, over the first nine months of the NHS, *went in six weeks*. Again indicates the state of the nation's health when so many had not been able to pay for treatment.

The decade of 1940-1950 saw major advances in the treatment of disease when the first antibiotics became available to everyone through the National Health Service. Before the discovery of penicillin, diseases and infections took their natural course and patients often died. When I started nursing in 1954, there was only penicillin and streptomycin available and these were used sparingly. They were given only by injection and hailed as wonder drugs.

Penicillin was discovered in 1928 but it was not until WW11 that it could be produced commercially and it was only used to treat wounded soldiers. This was also the case for streptomycin discovered in 1943. Streptomycin was the first drug to be effective against tuberculosis which was until then untreatable with 33 thousand deaths a year. It was a key discovery of the twentieth century. Prior to its discovery, TB treatment was isolation in a Sanatorium, bed rest, fresh air and a good diet. Both penicillin and streptomycin were not available for the general population until the start of the NHS in 1948.

Good nursing care and the careful dressing of infected wounds was the most important treatment for recovery from operations and chronic diseases.

Gradually new antibiotics started to appear. Today there are literally hundreds of different types available. The first *antibiotic resistant* strains of bacteria were isolated in 1946 and now resistant strains of bacteria are common. They are the source of world-wide hospital acquired infections. When Dad had his stomach removed, surgery was the only treatment for gastric ulcers. In 1982 scientists discovered that the ulcers were caused by a bacterium, helicobacter pylori. Since then, a course of antibiotics cures the disease. No need for massive surgery. *That really is an advance.*

Vaccination for smallpox has been available since the 1800s but even in 1950 there were still many cases. I remember my mother telling me not to stare at a man who had a terribly scarred and disfigured face. She explained that the scars were 'pock' marks from the disease and how sad it was and that he would have been very ill. People were really afraid of getting smallpox because if they survived, they would be disfigured and sometimes blind. I thought how awful to have your face changed so permanently.

Smallpox was a contagious disease, caused by a virus for which there was no treatment. In 1798 Edward Jenner discovered that inoculation with cowpox could protect against smallpox. The UK began a programme of inoculation and 1967 the World Health Organisation launched an intensified plan and today smallpox has been eradicated worldwide.

Polio, or infantile paralysis, was around for thousands of years but in the 1940s, summer epidemics in Britain became regular events. In the 1950s, the numbers reached forty-five thousand and hundreds died. Polio is a highly infectious disease caused by a virus affecting the central nervous system. It can cause totally irreversible paralysis in hours, and death if the breathing muscles are immobilized. The iron lung was used to treat survivors whose lungs were paralysed. The whole body was encased in a machine in which pressure was lowered and raised, causing the lungs to expand and contract. There is no treatment for the disease and some patients lived the rest of their lives in iron lungs or respirators. Some required crutches, special braces or wheelchairs in order to move around.

I nursed patients in the first iron lungs in the Churchill Hospital in Oxford and remember the terrible despair of patients as they realised they would never breath alone, or walk again. There is no treatment for the disease, but when the 'Salk' vaccine was developed in the 1950s, polio was brought under control and seasonal epidemics dropped. The changes during these years were momentous and came thick and fast as massive leaps were taken from poverty and deprivation into a welfare state that benefited all.

I feel tremendously privileged to have started nursing at such an important time in the NHS and to have been part of many thrilling changes.

23

THE BIG FREEZE 1947

Jan 28th — Heavy falls of snow, temperature down to 20F in Birmingham.
Feb 2nd — Snow fell early morning until late afternoon in Birmingham.
Feb 4th — Britain swept by blizzards, Midlands blocked, villages cut off.

These were just some of the reports in a Birmingham newspaper which said that in eighteen days a million tons of snow fell on Birmingham and that the Corporation had removed 30 thousand tons. How they measured a million tons, I don't know. On Thursday 23 January 1947, the snow started to fall. Snow on snow, deep and drifting fell from January to Easter.

There were no weather forecasts as we know them today. As far as I remember, we weren't expecting the huge amount of snow that fell overnight five days later on 28 January.

It was dark when Dad locked the door and said 'All's in that matters. I think it will snow again tonight.' We drew nearer the fire; it was cosy inside.

I woke next morning knowing something was different. I opened my eyes and the room was icy cold and strangely bright. There was not a sound, everything was hushed, no traffic sounds and no clip-clop of the horse as the milk and bread were delivered. Just silence and intense whiteness. Whatever was it?

I jumped out of bed and shivered on the icy lino floor. I was awestruck by what I saw. My world had been transformed. The hedges around the gardens had disappeared during the night; the tops of the trees seemed to stick out of a white blanket which enveloped houses right up to the window sills. Corners and angles had disappeared and were softened by gentle drifts. It was breath-taking. Snow was piled high in places and up and down the road it was impossible to get out of doors. Several foot of snow had fallen overnight and made a new and unfamiliar landscape. It was a winter wonderland. Clean white untrodden snow stretched in every direction.

I realised why I had woken. Dad was trying to open the door against a drift of snow and a huge icicle three or four-foot-long was hanging from the lintel. He started to clear the path—but where could he put the snow in this vast white wilderness? And what was the point of clearing a path that led to nowhere?

The snow brought chaos nationwide. Drifts were made higher by the snow that was cleared to the roadsides. Snow brought down telephone and electricity cables. Unpredicted electricity cuts were widespread. Coal was already in short supply; but now stocks were stuck at collieries because road and rail routes were blocked by snow. The world came to a halt. No bread or milk deliveries, no postman, no school at first. It was days before a semblance of life started again. For weeks in those freezing months, from January to March, we walked to school over the tops of the garden hedges; because they provided a firmer footing. We forgot the shape of the landscape underneath because everything was levelled by the snow.

Because there was no double glazing, Jack Frost traced beautiful patterns on the windows. Feathery ferns, icy swirls and glittering stars—you never knew what would appear as the air froze onto windows. I remember Dad saying, 'Jack Frost's been here again,' and as a small child I thought he was a real person. He is relegated now to transforming car windows with one off designs. . . a type of nature 'Banksey'.

'Do we have to go to school?' It was so cold there. The pipes had burst and the heating had broken down—or the caretaker hadn't enough coal. We wore extra clothes and, if we could get away with it, went to bed with our clothes on.

'But my legs are sore from my wellingtons.' But that wasn't a good excuse not to go to school. Legs got chafed by the tops of ugly black wellingtons and we were tired of wet clothes that constantly needed to be dried in front of the fire—if it was lit.

I can't remember if we ran out of coal and I can't remember how Mum got food from shops, which were themselves cut off from suppliers. There were no food stocks in the house because of rationing, and it was impossible to dig up vegetables which were frozen into the ground below mountains of snow.

Snow fell every day for fifty-five days and the temperature didn't rise above freezing for two months. The Met Office reported that thousands of people were cut off in their villages by snow-drifts 21 foot deep. Supplies had to be flown in by helicopter and the armed forces were called in to help clear roads and railways. Rivers were frozen and there were blocks of ice in the sea. This continued throughout February; but March brought even heavier blizzard conditions with continual heavy snow falls and strong gales.

The icicles that year were spectacular, hanging long and thick from roof eaves. When we did get into school, my teacher taught us a poem by William Shakespeare. I remember it every time it snows. *'When icicles hang by the wall and Dick the shepherd blows his nail, and Tom bears logs into the hall, and milk comes frozen home in pail.'*

The big freeze of 1947 was just two years after the war ended. The UK economy was still very weak. There were food and fuel shortages and houses had *no central heating, no insulation and no double glazing.* A week after the freeze began, the Minister of Fuel and Power, Emmanuel Shinwell, ordered electricity supplies to be cut to industry. Domestic electricity supplies were to be *turned off for five hours each day,* to conserve coal stocks. The penalty for using electricity during restricted times was a fine of one pound or three months in jail.

Five hours a day without electricity and empty coal sheds, increased the misery in every single home; many businesses including the House of Commons, were apparently reduced to working by candlelight. But the coal position was chaotic, long before the bad weather started.

'This country is facing a situation of unparalleled gravity.' Warned the MP for Southport opening a debate in the House of Commons.

He called for an account into the lack of foresight and action, on the part of the Government. Angry debates on the fuel crisis continued for days. The Government knew it was essential to accumulate large stocks of coal during the summer in order to avoid a breakdown during the winter. Various members said that the Minister, Emmanuel Shinwell, was warned repeatedly in the summer about the perilously low stock position and the inevitable consequences. He had not responded by taking adequate steps to build up stocks.

Warnings had also come during the summer from gas and electricity companies, saying that the coal position was very serious; that it might be necessary during the coming winter to reduce supplies. Industry also warned that hundreds of factories would be closed.

The worst did happen. The country froze. Factories closed and men were laid off. Four million workers were made idle by power cuts to industries. Coal trains could not get to power stations because of deep drifts on the railway lines and stocks were blocked at collieries. There were transport difficulties, food shortages, five hours a day of power cuts, deaths and illness from the cold.

For weeks it seemed that the sun hardly rose before it was setting again. That is if there was any sun. According to the Met Office, Birmingham had twenty-eight consecutive days without any sun at all. Every time we looked out of the window, fat whirling, twirling dancing snowflakes, could be seen against heavy grey skies. Even we children got fed up with the snow and the cold.

But we built snowmen that actually lasted. And one Sunday morning Dad helped us build an igloo in the garden. We cut blocks of frozen snow and piled them up and shaped them. We had completed it by lunchtime. It was five-foot-high and we thought it looked like a genuine Eskimo igloo.

'Can we have our dinner in it?'

'No, come inside and have it, it's warm indoors.' Mum dissuaded us and we ate our meal looking at it out of the window. We were listening to Cliff Mitchelmore and Jean Metcalfe on 'Two-Way Family Favourites.' They broadcast live every Sunday from London and Hamburg simultaneously. Musical requests for servicemen and their families were played over the radio.

'Oh no.' While we were looking, the igloo collapsed.'

'That's just where you would have been sitting,' Dad laughed, 'Never mind it was fun.'

The freeze finally ended at Easter and the country limped back to a form of normal but was then faced with floods from melting snow. The summer that followed was hot and idyllic. But it was also the summer of the polio epidemic that caused such panic across the nation. I know Mum worried about us; but so little was known about it that all she could do was worry.

In the spring following the big freeze, Christian Dior introduced his 'New Look.' Women were tired of the drab and restricted fashions of wartime when hems were short and trimmings few. The new fashions were glamorous and flattering with longer hemlines, nipped in waists and fuller skirts. The new fashion, however, was frowned upon by the government and people were discouraged from wearing clothes that 'wasted' so much fabric.

The advice was ignored by many women, especially as Princess Elizabeth and Princess Margaret were soon wearing the New Look. In the end, many designers copied it, responding to the public's desire for change.

I was ten in May and growing up. I still wanted toys for Christmas but was torn now between toys and clothes. The next year, to my surprise, it was just clothes that I wanted, I had grown out of toys. I was beginning to look at Mum's Woman's Weekly when I had the chance, with its fashion and beauty tips. But I wasn't too grown up to still read about my heroine in the Girls Crystal. Kay's adventures at a 'co-ed' school sounded very exciting.

24

DIVERGING PLANS

Our world was changing at every level. Those changes were coming rapidly in terms of the new NHS, the nationalisation of so many industries and the Education Act. A fairer society was needed and slowly it was emerging. Dad was still working for the Housing Department and must have been excited by the plans for the redevelopment of the city.

Mum however, had other interests. A plan was germinating in her mind. It may have been germinating for some time, but I can't remember it being talked about.

One day when I got home from school, I called, 'Mum where are you?'

'In here,' she was in the front room.

'What's that?' she was standing by a very large trunk, 'What's that for?'

'We're going to Australia.' She was smiling and laughing, 'We're going to see Grandad.'

She said we were emigrating to Australia. We were going on the £10 scheme that allowed people to go and return after two years if they weren't happy.

They kept talking about it and Mum started packing the trunk over the weeks. I was really excited. It would be a chance to see Mum's family. I remember skipping to school and telling my teacher. The plans were reinforced by the bitterly cold winter of 1947, which apparently prompted a flood of emigrations to that country.

I kept asking what would happen next but nothing seemed to happen. Eventually, Mum said we weren't going after all. Dad had another perforated stomach ulcer and I remember was really ill again for weeks. We learned much later that he didn't want to emigrate and dreaded the thought of being on board a ship for five or six weeks. The anxiety and worry had made him ill. Apart from which, the new society he had longed for, was happening here in Britain.

Mum was bitterly disappointed, she wanted to see her family again; even speaking on the phone to Australia cost £20 for three minutes and that was out of the question. She began to realise that she would never see them again and at times was really depressed. Her life had been one of loss. . .of family. . . of babies. . .of hopes for a better life. The war had finally taken its toll on her. She always made the best of every situation but when she was in her eighties, I asked her if life had been happy.

'No not really,' she replied, 'it wasn't what I thought it would be, but even so—I would never have been without you girls, you are my treasures.'

Dad had his own losses and deep disappointments but would never have wanted Mum to be unhappy. This was an impossible situation which could never be resolved.

So for the being time we stayed where we were. Dad embarked on DIY. It seems that a new fashion in decorating started after the war, everyone was refurbishing their property. Dad decided he wanted to 'stain and grain' all the woodwork. Perhaps it was the fore-runner of the fashion of stripping pine in order to see the wood grain.

He stripped off all the old paint and then painted on a thick wood coloured varnish. Whilst it was still tacky, he used a graining comb to make wavy lines, which were supposed to imitate wood grain. He varied the patterns, sometimes straight, sometimes wavy, until he finished all the doors. He then started on the staircase. Carpets were narrower than the stairs in those days, so he painstakingly did the risers too. Every bit of woodwork in the house was stained and grained. It seems every house in those days, had the same pale brown, stained and grained woodwork which became characteristic of the decade. The finished effect did not seem like wood to me but Dad was proud of his work.

In the next house we moved to, the fashion was different. All the paintwork was white but Dad told us he was going to paint all the doors upstairs a different colour. One door I remember was purple and one, I think pink but the others I forget.

Now that the war was over we went on holiday again. There were no credit or debit cards, so money for the holiday was withdrawn from the Post Office and carried in cash. In fact, everything we needed for a day out was carried with us. Mum in my memory, always seemed to be loaded down with bags. *She was the original 'bag lady.'*

One year we went to Pendine in South Wales. We stayed for the first time in a caravan near to the beach. It belonged to a friend of Dad, who offered it to us for a week. It was very quiet, without any other caravans and close to the village. Dad's friend met us when we arrived and showed us the caravan.

'This isn't big enough,' thought Dad, 'But we can't all get in here.' he said to his friend.

'Don't worry Bill,' said the caravan owner, 'come with me.' The caravan was in a field and next to it was a big marquee which must have been used for village activities. 'I've put you a bed in here, in the marquee.'

Dad was puzzled, this wasn't what he had expected. When his friend had gone he said,

'I'm not sleeping in there.' It was pouring down with typical 'Welsh' rain and Dad hated tents and camping anyway. He shuddered and said he would sleep on the floor of the caravan. It was a squash. That night it rained and rained; it thundered and lightning struck all night long. The wind blew at gale force and during the night we heard a crashing sound. The central pole of the marquee had come down bringing the whole marquee with it.

Next morning Dad looked at the damage and said 'That pole is exactly where I would have been sleeping!' It had a 10-inch diameter. He said he would never have another caravan holiday.

Dad loved holidays with his family. He was very much aware of how different our lives were to his own childhood years. Now that he was working for the City Council, he had to take turns with all the other employees for holiday dates. He was allowed two weeks and needed to apply for the weeks he wanted; then wait and see what he was allotted. Sometime it wasn't even in the summer.

I remember him saying, 'Never mind, I promise we'll go out for days instead.'

One day trip stands out. We went to the Lake District for the day and were so excited. The Lakes sounded romantic and mysterious. We went off very early one Sunday morning on the train. The railways were advertising day trips at the cost of £1 return, including a cruise on Lake Windermere. It was a very long day and Mum packed picnics and clothes and whatever was needed. The train arrived at Windermere station and after a time in the town, we went for the cruise on a Steamer on the Lake. It was 1am when we arrived back in Birmingham, very tired but very happy.

That year we had ice cream which began to appear again after the war from men riding 'Stop me and buy one' trikes. The ice cream was wrapped in white paper, which had to be removed. There were little blocks of ice cream, slightly bigger that a match box, to go with wafers and round blocks for the cones.

One Sunday Dad said, 'Girls, would you like to go all round on the Outer Circle 11?' He often took us out at weekends, whilst Mum stayed at home for a rest.

'Yes please, when can we go.'

'This afternoon.'

'Yippee, all the way round, how long will it take?'

'About two hours, I think, but you won't be able to get off 'til we get back home.'

This was really exciting. We climbed the stairs and sat on the front seat of the bus and went all round the 26-mile circle of the suburbs. Dad pointed out the interesting places and enjoyed it as much as we did. I learned later that lots of other Birmingham children did the same. Over the years, wherever we needed to go, it seems we caught the Outer Circle 11, it was part of daily life.

The Outer Circle bus route, came in to operation in April 1926. In the 1930s, the route was so popular with the public, that half-day holiday trips were advertised as competition to the trams to the Lickey Hills! This iconic route has become part of Birmingham's heritage.

The Birmingham Mail wrote in 2012 that more than 50 thousand commuters use the No 11 route each day, which has 272 stops, serves 40 pubs, 69 leisure facilities, 233 schools, 19 retail centres and six hospitals. The Mail was inundated with memories of thousands of folk who had travelled the Circle. My own strange tale of the dark blue and yellow Number 11, is later on in this story.

For a while there was an annual nostalgia trip on vintage buses doing the circuit. And how about the memorabilia. . .chopping boards and trays, jigsaws of the route, calendars and drinks coasters all celebrating the number 11. And who wouldn't want a mouse mat with,

'Today I am in Brummie heaven on the Outer Circle 11', designed by Kevin Beresford of 'Whacky Roundabouts'.

The Lickey Hills are also very special. Some of the best memories of childhood are days that we took a picnic to the Lickey Hills. On Bank Holiday Monday, it seemed the whole of Birmingham was out for the day. We caught the number 70 tram in Selly Oak and excitedly climbed the narrow winding stairs to the top. With a loud noise, a jerk and a ring of the bell, the tram moved off down the track, swinging from side to side as it gathered speed.

The tram along the Bristol Road, ran down a beautiful tree-lined track that seemed a foretaste of the countryside to come. . .Bristol, that name always drew me. I wanted to go there even as a child. *Bristol, the end of land, and the beginning of the sea and the beginning of rest of the world.* It seemed a perfect place to live. I wanted to drive right down Bristol Road and get on a ship to exotic places.

Instead, we piled off at the terminal in Rednal. There were often crowds of people but the woods and hills seemed big enough to absorb them all. We climbed up the endless wooden steps, racing ahead of Mum and Dad shouting 'Come on, hurry up.' We walked for miles, picnicked and played in the woods until we were tired. Those woods in springtime were a haze of stunning blue and the delicate perfume from carpets of bluebells wafted on the air.

There was an amusement arcade near the terminal but we never had money to spend there, although sometimes we would buy a drink. A favourite drink or 'pop' from those days was Ice Cream Soda or Dandelion and Burdock. After the war, the Corona man delivered pop to our home every week. We were allowed three bottles and got 2d back for the empties. I think the name 'pop' came from the fact that the drinks were very fizzy. It was difficult in those days to make a top that would stay on and keep the fizz in place. Corona invented a sort of metal spring that 'popped' the top off when it was pushed.

At the end of the day in the hills, there was always a mad dash for the trams to try to get ahead of the endless queues that stretched along the road. Sometimes we were waiting long after dark, but everyone was good natured and there always seemed to be enough trams to take everyone home—eventually. Today the hills are designated a Country Park covering 500 acres of woods and heath-land, with a Visitor Centre and Park Rangers. It has been a Birmingham treasure to countless generations of Brummies.

Birmingham trams were very attractive and narrower than those in many cities. The city streets were narrow, which meant both trams and tracks were narrower than usual. They were dark blue and primrose double-deckers, with bright adverts on the sides. Many trams had open balconies upstairs with slatted wooden seats.

The driver stood at the front and used a sort of wheel handle to control the tram. On a return journey, the tram didn't turn round; the trolley pole was swung round to the back by the driver and hooked onto the overhead power cables. That brings back powerful memories—the sight of the driver swinging and hooking the cable. The driver then went to the wheel at the other end which was now the front. Tram seats were reversible and the conductor, who took the fares, reversed the seats for the return. He came round after each stop saying 'fares please' and having received the fare would punch a ticket. The last tram ran to the Lickeys in 1952 and the last City tram ran in 1953. It was the end of an era lasting fifty years that still holds special affection for many Birmingham folks.

25

THE DELL

After the Big Freeze we had a swelteringly hot summer. We spent all our time outdoors. As children, we lived from day to day, not realising how rapidly life was changing in post-war Britain. Unlike our parents, we had already forgotten the horrors of war which ended so recently. Our lives consisted of school and play. When Dick Barton, Special Agent, arrived in 1946, it became the new craze.

At 6:45pm, from Monday to Friday, came the summons 'Dick Barton's on.'

With that, it seemed that all children everywhere, disappeared indoors.

'Quick, it's started.' Mum was primed to tell us the minute it came on. At 7pm we were out again, to have adventures of our own play-acting Dick, Snowy and Jock and imitating their daring escapades.

We had no television and very few toys but the radio was powerful entertainment. It is hard to imagine life without a television or computers, iPods and mobile phones to keep in constant touch with friends. We had none of these, so entertainment was based in simple home activities. Families would often spend the evening listening to the radio or wireless together. We listened as a family to serialisations of Lorna Doone and Jane Eyre and I especially remember the Forsyte Saga which was a favourite with Mum and Dad. Our imaginations responded to the 'told story' in a way impossible with television. At some time, the Archers started and became 'must hear' serial that developed a 20,000,000 audience.

I remember too the way we all laughed at Much Binding in the Marsh with Kenneth Horne and Richard Murdoch. The fact that they were just standing in front of a mike, with home-made props for sound effects, didn't dawn on us then. For children there was 'Children's Hour' and 'Toy-town' and Uncle Mac; but we also listened to the News which always began with something like: 'Here is the News and this is Alvar Liddell reading it: Yesterday one hundred allied bombers raided Germany.'

As we grew up, we gained more freedom and in the summer holidays we were out all day. It was safer in those days and parents were not worried as long as we were back for meals. One place we escaped to for hours was the Dell. The Dell was damp, mysterious and fascinating.

One day, one of Mary's friends said, 'Let's go to the Dell.'

'Yes let's.' The verdict was unanimous.

It was about three quarters of a mile away—we hopped, skipped and raced to get there. One of the girls was pushing an empty pram at full speed.

'Mum said if I went to the Dell I was to bring back some firewood.'

When we arrived at the Dell, we noticed there were horses in the next field. What a good place to collect the manure that Dad wanted for his tomatoes. He was passionate about his tomatoes. Tomatoes needed manure. The horses that drew the milk delivery carts, obligingly delivered manure if you were quick enough to get it. In the holidays Dad's instructions were to watch for the horses and left us a metal bucket and shovel. We didn't seem to mind in those days; but then all the children were doing the same thing.

We played in the wood for a long time. Exploring and chasing one another until I got stuck in a bog. My feet were sinking deeper and deeper into soft black mud. Suddenly I realised that we had strayed into a wet and damp area and bogs stretched in every direction. I couldn't reach the little grassy path that I stepped off.

'Help,' I shouted, 'get me out.' Every time I drew one foot out, the other went down further.

'Catch this,' someone shouted and held out a broken branch.

'I can't reach it,' my leg went down to the knee in bog. The others terrified me, they told me that sometimes people got stuck in bogs and were sucked right under. Somehow or another they rescued me. My shoes squelched and one came off in the bog as I was pulled out.

'I know. . .you can sit in the pram.' said the pram owner. I was splashed in thick black mud right up to my knees and I was cold. I sat in the pram, my feet dangling over the side and watched the others play, the mud dried on my legs and hands. Then they pushed me home minus a shoe.

I don't know what Mum said about our escapade but she was always philosophical so in the probably in the end, 'It's no use crying over spilt milk—but be careful next time.'

We went back the next day with two metal buckets and a shovel. Of course we played in the woods again; but this time we carefully avoided the bogs. Finally, we went into the field and collected two full buckets of manure and started home. Mary and I carried the buckets but they were they were old fashioned grey metal and were heavy and we were tired.

'Let's go on the bus', said Mary, 'I've got some money.' What a good idea.

We waited at the number 11 bus stop near Sarehole Mill. The bus came and we climbed aboard and sat in a row on the long seat, just inside the door. We all sat together with the two buckets balanced between us. The smell in the heat of the bus was terrible!

'Hey, you can't have that on here', said the conductor coming down the bus, 'you'll have to get off.'

'Please, we've only got another stop.' By then we were nearly home, so he just shrugged.

'Well it's the next stop or I'll ring the bell.'

Mum and Dad couldn't believe what we had done. At least Dad was pleased with the manure. I am horrified when I think about it now.

Although more than sixty years ago, I could remember exactly where the Dell was; but it is only when I checked on Google recently, that I learned it was the same wood that inspired Tolkien to write the 'Lord of the Rings' in 1948. Perhaps Tolkien was wandering in the woods when I was stuck in the bog in 1947. Perhaps I was his inspiration.

'The marshes and bogs had spread wider and wider on either side. Paths had vanished, and many a rider and wanderer too, if they had tried to find the lost ways across.' Hobbit chap 10.

That sounds just like I experienced—bogs spread wider and wider and paths vanished. In his childhood, J. R. Tolkien lived near that same Dell. He said he played there and it was the inspiration for the mystical woods in his books. *'It was a kind of lost paradise. . .there was a wonderful dell with flowers.'* The Dell is now the Moseley Bog Nature Reserve.

We were growing fast and becoming more independent with interests of our own. I was ten in 1947 and there were so many things I wanted to do and be. I wanted to be a nurse but at the same time I would like to be a teacher and definitely an explorer or an inventor. On the other hand, I wanted to be an artist. I wanted to do all these and lots more at the same time, it was a bit confusing.

I especially wanted to be a writer. I had a secret hiding place under a floor board for the stories I wrote. It was the perfect, mysterious place to hide something as exciting as my adventure story. Just knowing it was there, a guarded secret, added a thrill to daily living. I couldn't wait to get home from school to write. This was going to be a big seller and make me famous. I didn't know about Tolkien; but perhaps the Dell inspired me in the same way it inspired him!

My book was about a girl—of course—whose brother was lost in China. China in the days after the war and without television, seemed an unknown mysterious country. My heroine set out to find her brother. I had reached the place where she pressed the eye of the idol in the temple—I think I probably got China and idols muddled up with Thailand and temples. The idol slowly moved to reveal. . .? Naturally, it was going to be fabulous treasure and would lead to her brother but I never wrote another word. This really is a sad tale about a tale.

One night I tiptoed downstairs to get a drink of water and stood, as children do, outside the living room door listening to whether it was OK to go in. Mum and Dad and my Aunt and Uncle were comfortably seated.

Aunt was saying, 'Go on then, I can't wait to hear the next instalment.'

'She hasn't written much this time,' Mum said, 'but this bit is good.' She was reading my story and it was interspersed with laughter and exclamations.

I felt stunned and embarrassed and went back to bed. And I really *was* embarrassed, in fact I was squirming. They had been reading my story, instalment by instalment as I wrote it. And why were they laughing—was it so stupid? How could they invade my private thoughts? I never wrote another word. When I look back I realise they weren't laughing at me. I just didn't know how to handle it. On the positive side I determined that when I had children, I would never read anything they left around. I didn't, diaries were sacrosanct and so were their letters.

Although I stopped writing, I never stopped daydreaming. I spent hours, with my elbows on the window sill, looking out and daydreaming about anything and everything. I was often told, 'Stop daydreaming and get on with something useful.' But daydreaming *was* useful. I was thinking. . .and that was useful. When my own children daydreamed, I knew exactly what they were doing and didn't stop them.

26

NOVEMBER ... FOGS AND A WEDDING

And so the year of 1947 ended. November was colder in those days. The bonfire nights I remember as a child were freezing cold. Dad used to tell us to wait indoors whilst he set up the fireworks. We dressed in several layers of clothes including woolen hats and gloves; still our fingers froze as we held the sparklers and watched them fizz and spit with golden showers. I loved Catherine wheels and sometimes we had a rocket but the range was limited, even when money was available.

November brought fogs. It wasn't just snow that caused havoc. 'Pea souper fogs' caused chaos and everything stopped, sometimes for days at a time. A fog could reduce visibility to a few feet and the air was wet and dirty causing asthma attacks. Hospital admissions rose dramatically. The fogs were caused when smoke and pollutants, from thousands of factories and domestic fires, built up in cold motionless air. A fog could last for days reducing visibility to a few feet and the air was wet and dirty. Buses stopped and people walked for hours in order to get home. Fog got into the nose and lungs and smelled sulphurous and suffocating.

To be enveloped in a dirty grey blanket, is totally disorientating. It was not unusual to hear someone, shout, 'Where am I'? That happened most often when a kerb ended and a road had to be crossed. Which way do you go and where are you when you arrive? Sometimes it was on the other side of the road, sometimes in the middle, with no way of finding the pavement. Add wartime blackout and the result was chaos.

One night, Dad got home at nearly midnight and we were all waiting up for him. 'We've been so worried.' said Mum, handing him a cup of tea.

Dad looked exhausted, 'I've been walking in front of a bus with a torch,' he flopped into a chair, 'the driver couldn't see the kerb and we had to show him where it was.' He had walked with the conductor just feet in front of the bus.

'I had to read out the names of roads so that passengers could get off at the right places.'

Sometimes buses mounted pavements or turned in the wrong direction. Drivers didn't turn back but just kept going. Dad walked miles out of his way that night.

I remember fog being so thick, that I could hardly see my hand in front of my face; the yellow glow of street lights mysteriously appearing and disappearing into the swirling mist. At times, employers sent staff home early because fog was descending and schools closed early so pupils could get home. Those were days without mobile phones but folks seemed to take things in their stride, it was a part of life.

The word SMOG was coined in the 1950s, to describe the fog caused by the combination of smoke and acid pollution from factory chimneys. All industrial cities had the same problem and more than two thousand people died in a London SMOG in 1952. Birmingham had been used to days of 'Dickensian' fogs for many years.

The Clean Air Act was passed in 1952 and required smokeless fuels to be used in designated smokeless zones. The fogs stopped after this and the reduction of smoke, also meant centuries of black soot and grime could be cleaned off buildings. What had seemed ugly towns, changed into beautiful desirable places to live.

 In the foggy winter of 1947, Princess Elizabeth married Prince Philip on November 20. It was the first ceremonial occasion for six years and the nation revelled in it. It brought new hope to post-war Britain. The Golden Coach carried the beautiful bride along the processional route, from Buckingham Palace to Westminster Abbey.

It was the first time a Royal wedding had been filmed and broadcast to millions listening at home. There were no cameras inside the Abbey but television cameras were positioned outside the Palace and the Abbey for live transmission. Richard Dimbleby narrated events as the Princess and her husband returned to Buckingham Palace in the Glass Coach. The newspapers said Elizabeth looked shy, but radiant and absolutely lovely.

Elizabeth did look beautiful in her Norman Hartnell dress, accompanied by eight bridesmaids and Philip was handsome in his naval uniform. Elizabeth's dress was of ivory silk, decorated with flowers and wheat ears picked out by ten thousand seed pearls. It was worked on for seven weeks in complete secrecy. She wore a 13-foot gossamer circular train and veil, fastened by a Russian tiara and carried a bouquet of orchids.

Philip renounced his Greek royal title, Prince Philip of Greece and Denmark, and became a naturalised British subject. Hours before the wedding, he was named His Royal Highness and created Duke of Edinburgh. There were few TVs in those days, so people packed cinemas to see the film footage and queued to look at wedding presents.

As the future Queen married her Prince, the British Empire was beginning to disintegrate. India became the first country to become independent. Before the war in 1935, the 'Government of India Act' attempted to create an elected Assembly. It failed because it ignored the religious rivalry between the Muslims and Hindus.

After the war, the newly elected Labour government appointed Lord Mountbatten, Prince Philip's uncle, as Viceroy. He concluded that peace could only be achieved if partition was introduced. In August 1947, the Indian Independence Act was signed. This created an independent state of India and an independent state of Pakistan.

Millions moved across the new frontiers, Hindus moved across to India, whilst Muslims in India, moved to Pakistan. Where the two moving groups met, violence occurred and it is thought that 250 thousand people were murdered in religious clashes. Two years later in 1949, the British Commonwealth was formally constituted. This established all member states as 'free and equal.' The King became the Head of the British Commonwealth of Nations.

27

GRAMMAR SCHOOL

Mum and Dad were both really keen that we should have the education they missed out on. I passed the 11 plus and started at Kings Norton Grammar School for Girls in 1948. Ann went in 1949. It was an unfair system but from a selfish point of view, I am grateful I had the opportunity to go. Possibly the most privileged of all generations; we were given the opportunities our parents were denied. That same year we moved to Harborne.

There are so many memories– the classrooms– the teachers– the lessons– the exams– gym slips and blazers–order marks for not wearing hats or for eating in the street–'Don't run in the corridor.'

But where do I begin? The first morning is shrouded in confusion— crowds of neatly dressed girls, purposefully going—but going where? How did I get to where I was going? In my mind's eye I can see the aerial perspective of the school, every bit of the layout and yet at the same time— in the curious way only memory enables—I can simultaneously walk through corridors and classrooms and through rapidly changing scenes.

The first instruction was clear; 'All pupils must use the lower entrance gates.'

The drive through those gates passed tennis courts on the right, veered left by the cycle sheds to a long wide promenade along the back of the school. Girls, girls and more girls everywhere. To use a 'today' expression it was awesome.

The promenade overlooked slopes down to hockey and rounder pitches;

and then on down more steep slopes to netball pitches fringed at the perimeter by tall poplars trees. It was an attractive school in extensive grounds. We spent our breaks on those open spaces, I still remember the smell of chocolate that wafted on the wind from close by Cadbury's Bournville Factory.

The promenade continued past the 'never to be forgotten sewing room', towards the dining room. I wonder how many girls made navy blue PE knickers in that sewing room for their very first sewing project. And knickers they were, unglamorous with elasticised legs and capacious enough to tuck gym slips into.

'Now girls, you are going to make PE knickers.' The Domestic Science Teacher measured us carefully. 'The length is from your waist down to your knees and two extra inches.'

'How horrible,' whispered one girl.

'You will make your knickers by hand, not on the sewing machine.'

We learned that this was so we could learn 'proper' stitching. On those knickers we learned the art of French seams, painfully stitched by hand, unstitched and stitched again and again, until so precise that they might as well have been machine stitched.

The top drive was out of bounds to lower school pupils. It led to the front entrance hall—'a sacred, never to be entered place without permission and then only on tiptoe and in silence,'—that forbidden place was the abode of the Headmistress. Both awe inspiring and frightening, she reigned from there.

So how did I get to 2B on my first day, and how did I find my way around those windy, open quadrangles? I suspect a prefect met and escorted us but I am not sure. I do remember the girls I met on the first of many memorable days. I remember too, their names on the register as it was recited daily for years. Sometime in those first days in September, we were orientated around the school, elected class monitors, dinner monitors and endless other monitors and learned about the prefects.

Prefects, awe-inspiring senior girls whose look sent us scurrying as fast as possible in the opposite direction. The fact that they were learning to accept responsibility, escaped eleven-year-olds. They were just a very effective spy system and their eyes and ears were everywhere, and they could give out *order marks. . .for disorder.*

In those first days we were taught to wear our school uniform with pride, always to wear our hats and never, *ever* be seen eating in the street in uniform. In fact, we were unified by navy gym slips or skirts, pale blue blouses, ties, blazers and the inevitable beret with the KNGS badge; and not to forget, the brown leather satchels which were never big enough for homework.

I found Grammar School very different to Primary School. We had timetables for lessons and had to remember where to go and to get there on time. The one hour of homework in the first year, increased to three hours by the time we left school. Pressures and expectations were high. It was about discipline, hard work and order. Latin, German, French, Classics Society, Voluntary Society, and every society imaginable. Dad was envious.

We played hockey and netball in the winter and tennis and rounders in the summer. I couldn't wait to get out onto the hockey pitch with my new hockey stick and whack the ball. I was sure I would be good. I was going to be a star, a champion. . .I was going to thwack that ball and I couldn't wait. I can feel even now the funny rubbery feel of the handle grip as I tensely held it in readiness.

For an hour we dribbled the ball down the length of the pitch and back, to the shout of, 'Keep the stick off the ground–dribble gently–continuously–no hitting–faster.'

What a bore. . .no thwacking and I did so want to thwack. But where would I have thwacked it? Who might I have hit? Then there was 'bullying off,' I just never got the ball. I stood bemused at how that girl, who was also good at dribbling, always snatched the ball away however hard I tried. Hockey was not to be my forte.

I lost interest, but I knew I would be good at netball. After all, my Girls Crystal heroines were good at it. Again I was disappointed. Again it was about disciplined learning of positions and 'passes.' Never mind, there was still rounders and tennis to come.

But I discovered I hated rounders. I missed the ball mostly and so eventually, I learned to 'bunk off' in the cloakrooms with other disillusioned sportswomen. We un-tucked our gymslips out of those dreadful knickers and talked about how to avoid being caught. Never mind. The locked cupboard in the corridor contained La Crosse sticks and we were promised we would learn that one day. Now I was sure to be good at that.

I did enjoy gym—but even there, those same girls who excelled on the hockey pitch and on the netball pitch, and at rounders, could climb right to top of the ropes whilst most of us were dangling halfway up. But as for folk dancing—I can still do the 'Paddy one-step.'

I joined the school choir and there I did well, I loved those times especially. We sang a very wide repertoire that included every sort of folk song, classical music, operettas etc. Sometimes, I find myself singing along with something on the radio—something I learned at school. I think I absorbed the classics through singing in the choir.

We learned Latin and French. Latin we were told, would lay a good foundation in our understanding of other languages. That was certainly true. I can still remember some of the Latin declensions we recited in unison.

Days began with assembly. Let no headmistress ever underestimate the power of words, even if they seem unheeded at the time. We were exhorted and expected to reach out for the impossible and a sense of pride in the school was installed. It was in the hall that great expectations for the future were inspired; it was also in the hall on Wednesday morning that lists of names for detention were read out. Four order marks = one detention—at least I managed to miss that.

That hall holds many memories, Christmas parties, PE on wet days, but especially neat rows of girls in blue blouses singing school hymns. And whenever I hear the music of 'Blaze Away' and 'All in a Country Garden,' a picture is triggered of row after row of girls getting up, and filing out in orderly fashion.

In 1948, the same year that I started at Kings Norton, my mother, with thousands of others, queued to collect new ration books. We were still affected by shortages and needed points for clothing and furniture. Mum had to find extra coupons for my school uniform. Sugar, sweets, butter and meat remained on ration until six years later. In that same year Mum was still doing the family washing in a tub with a dolly peg and wringing the washing with the old fashioned mangle.

In my last year at school, the King died in his sleep on Wednesday 6 February, 1952. He was fifty-six and had suffered with cancer of the lung for some time. We heard the news at school in the middle of the morning. We were moving between lessons and one of the girls came in crying, 'The King has died.' We didn't know what to believe and the tension increased by the minute. At around eleven-thirty, the school was summoned to assemble in the Hall where it was confirmed that he had died.

Sadness and grief was felt throughout the school. The King had been an amazing support for the nation during the war, refusing to leave London even during the darkest time. He was out around the country inspecting damage and comforting with his presence throughout. We were old enough to remember those times.

Princess Elizabeth was in Kenya with Prince Philip. When she returned she was Queen. The Headmistress exhorted us all to aspire to new heights as 'New Elizabethans'. We were, she said, at the start of a wonderful new era and as post-war children had been given great privileges. . .we were to seize them and take every opportunity presented. We were inspired.

Unfortunately, after a good start for my first year and a good report, I discovered a social life. Life *outside* school was exciting and fun. . .so much fun that I couldn't concentrate *inside* school. From 1950, all I could think and daydream about was the Youth Club at the local church, and all the kids that made up 'the crowd.' Nevertheless, the headmistress did inspire me with talk about 'New Elizabethans.'

And Dad said—'You will regret not working, I wish I could go back to school'.

28

YOUTH CLUB

For three years I was totally absorbed with my friends at the Youth Club and it happened by chance. I was with a friend in the library one evening, whispering and looking for books when two boys approached.

One of them said, 'A man wants to speak to you two.' It was as abrupt as that.

'What do you mean, a man wants to talk to us?' We recognised the boys from the church that we both went to. 'What does he want to talk about?'

'Come and see.'

We were curious, so we followed them giggling to some rooms in the village. The mystery was explained. . .A couple from St Peter's church had just started a youth club and that night were wondering how to increase membership. The boys—I can't remember their names—said they knew where girls from the church would be, and were sent to fetch us.

'So' they said, 'Would you like to join?'—Of course we would.

Youth clubs were fairly new in those days and we felt very 'avant-garde.' I explained airily to Mum and Dad that 'everyone' went to a Youth Club. They were totally bemused. The following week we took several other friends and the next week they brought more. Eventually, around forty or more of us met every Friday night in those small rooms. That was the beginning and it took over and became my life for the next few years.

There was a snooker table, a piano and a small kitchen. Room to play games, a few chairs and a platform. I first heard jazz from that piano, and it was there I learned to 'rock and roll.' We watched the snooker but mostly just chatted. It was fun and our school friends were envious and wanted to join. School was relegated to second place.

The Goon Show was a big craze and the boys role-played the characters, repeating for us that week's performance. We had our own Eccles and Bluebottle, a Moriarty and of course Bloodnock who repeatedly said 'you deaded me.' We laughed hysterically at mining for socks in Woolworth's basement and surfacing in Australia. We all had the 'lurgi,' invented by Spike Milligan, which has become part of our language today; and we sang or intoned the Ying–Tong Song.

The 'crowd' went everywhere together. There were parties for birthdays, for Christmas and any other opportunity and some parents allowed us to use their homes. We had a tramp party and dressed like tramps with rolled up trousers, saucepans hanging from our waists and soot on our faces. We went to other church youth clubs to their 'church hops.' We did the Lambeth Walk and the Palais Glide to a great deal of laughter and noise. We waltzed and foxtrotted and rocked and rolled.

Sometimes we went to the pictures together, if we could afford it, the 'Royalty Picture Palace' in Harborne was up-market and cost 1s 6d in the stalls. . .or if we were short of money it was the 'Flea Pit'. I don't think it was a pit of fleas, just scruffier and cheaper. Why do teenagers need to give everything and everyone nicknames? We certainly did.

There was swimming and tennis and walks on bank holidays. Boys and girls paired off and went out with each other in turn, but always in the safety of the group. Wherever one went, all went. If there was no Youth Club, we met outside the Gas Offices in the village. The forecourt of the brightly lit showrooms became our meeting place. It must have been irritating to see dozens of youngsters, often on bikes, talking, shouting and messing around for hours.

So what's changed. . .?

We were like the kids in 'Happy Days.' Emerging teenagers who hadn't yet been given that title. . .daring to do things differently, not carbon copies of our parents as in previous generations. As for my parents who worried about my homework, I always managed to convince them it was done. *And Dad said as usual—'You will regret not working, I wish I could go back to school'.*

The 50s decade brought new teenage fashions that were cheap to buy or easy to make. I made lots of things—after I had done my homework! My favourite was a circular skirt in royal blue, I wore three bouffant net petticoats underneath to make it stand out. It was great for rocking and rolling. But I needed money for those new fashions, so when I was fourteen, I started work on Saturdays in a hairdressing salon.

I swept the floor, made the tea and handed the hairdresser the curlers for perms. I will never forget the electric machine that was used to perm hair. Strands of hair were soaked in lotion that smelled strongly of ammonia; the hair was then carefully rolled around a heavy metal roller. When all hair had been rolled, each roller was attached by a lead to an electric heater overhead. Thirty or forty leads were connected to the heating machine. The client was left attached for at least three hours 'heating' the perm. It looked scary. The final perm looked like corrugated waves pushed into symmetrical lines.

Our next door neighbour was in her late teens and her hair was a mass of bubbly curls. I asked her how she did it. She set her hair in pin curls, winding a small strand of hair around her finger and clipping it tight to her head. She made forty pin curls every single night. In the morning her hair was curly but there was no hair spray to fix it, so the damp and rain straightened it.

Finally, home-perms arrived on the scene. A kit contained little rubber rollers and cold perm lotion which took less than an hour to complete. Toni home perms were possibly the most popular. Everybody saw the picture of identical twins with identical hairstyles and the marketing jingle 'Which twin has the Toni'. It was intended to make permed curls look so natural that you couldn't see which twin had the perm. I tried one several times. Dad always complained about the smell of ammonia that affected the house for days.

For weeks and weeks, a puzzling advert was seen on the corner of Bristol Road in Selly Oak. Spread across the corner was a huge hoarding with, 'AMAMI is coming,' spelled out in gigantic letters.

'What on earth is AMAMI?' we all said repeatedly. How strange, no-one knew. Eventually the advert changed to AMAMI is nearly here.

'I wish it would hurry and come,' said Dad.

Finally, we saw, 'Friday night is AMAMI night.' Then we understood, Friday night was the traditional night when girls stayed in to wash their hair. Amami was a new styling lotion, to be used on Friday nights. The advert certainly attracted attention and of course I tried it.

I will always remember one memorable Christmas when I was fourteen. Presents by now were the requested clothes. An Aunt gave me a package, about 10 x 8 inches, wrapped in Christmas paper. I took off the paper to see a thin cardboard box; and nestled in folds of tissue inside was my first pair of nylon stockings. They were fully fashioned, 30 denier with a seam down the back. Charnos, Wolsley and Kayser are names I remember and they cost 10/6 ... ten shillings and sixpence in old money. Now I needed a suspender belt or girdle ... made of cotton, lightweight and with four suspenders to anchor the stockings.

I loved the sound of church bells. I often looked inside the small door in the bell tower at St Peter's. . .I would love to ring those bells. Eventually, with a friend, I did just that. The Ringing Master was delighted to get some young people involved, and so I became a teenage campanologist. The other ringers were mostly elderly and we were thoroughly spoiled. We went to our first ringing practice at six-thirty, one Monday night. As we climbed the narrow spiral stone staircase to the bell tower, the sound of bells got ever more deafening.

There were eight huge bells in the tower. From each bell, hanging in an upper chamber, there was a long rope which finished in a multi-coloured sally—the fluffy, woolly, hand held part of the rope.

'The bells have to be pulled gradually from hanging down until they are facing up and ready to ring.' explained the ringing Master. 'Hold the sally and try how it feels, never let go of the sally or you will break the bell stay up there.'

The thought of that was scary, it sounded as if those great heavy bells were perched precariously, ready to crash down with one careless move. The heaviest bell, the tenor, weighed more than half a ton.

With his hand over mine, he let me feel the power of the bell as it was gently but firmly pulled into place. It felt heavy but easy as he got into rhythm.

'And that's the lightest bell, the treble.' I watched as the other bells were pulled up and a peal started.

I learned to ring a straight peal but I could never get the hang of ringing the changes.

No one explained properly and the Master kept saying, 'Just follow that bell that goes before you, he knows what to do and you just follow.'

That meant watching to see which sally was moving immediately before mine. I couldn't get the hang of it. The 'one going before me', kept changing around the room. I couldn't keep up with the changes. It was amazing watching those ropes flying, hands, arms and coloured sallies going up and down in turn.

We went on several ringing trips with the team to other churches. There was a camaraderie and a competition between ringers as to how many churches and which bells they had rung. Stories were told about who had broken a stay and which bells were difficult to ring, where the biggest and heaviest bell was. Just like fisherman claiming the biggest catch.

A surprising number of expressions originated in bell ringing. 'Ringing the changes'– 'going like the clappers'–'getting the hang of it'–'dropping a clanger.'

Eventually, one of the boys learned we were afraid of walking through the graveyard after ringing practice and came to meet us. The rest found out, and before long the whole gang was waiting for us to finish. It was something for them to do. The noise from their shouting and laughter could be heard in the bell tower and eventually the Master would say,

'It's time for you to go, your friends are here.'

In time, the noise and disruption got too much and we gave up bell ringing. But I shall never forget, 'Here's gone one', the call given as the first bell rang.

Even without mobile phones, we always knew where everyone was. We thought we were the best and the wittiest and the cleverest and that no other young people ever had the fun we had. We were no different from any other group but we probably thought we were. We certainly had a wonderful time. I saw a sticker on the back of someone's car–

'Employ young people whilst they still know everything.' *We were very employable.*

Meanwhile my schoolwork suffered. . .Monday bell ringing. . .Tuesday swimming. . .Thursday library. . .Friday youth club. . .Saturday whatever . . .Sunday church. . .Perhaps you could say it was 'social education'.

29

I AM A TEENAGER

I didn't know I was a teenager. . .the name hadn't been invented. . .It was the fifties. . .I didn't know it would be fabulous. . .I didn't know it would be a wonderful decade of freedom and increasing prosperity. . .I didn't know how privileged we were. It was a 'gay' time! Gay meaning vivacious, jaunty, effervescent, smiling, cheerful, sparkling, joyful! A good word, it's a pity we can't use it.

 I became an actual teenager in 1950. For my thirteenth birthday I was given a silver grey Coventry Eagle bicycle and I was allowed to choose it. A beautiful soft silver colour. I washed, cleaned, polished and cherished it every day. I don't know why Mum and Dad decided to spend so much money on a bike for me. I hadn't asked, I knew money was short, but I was so thrilled.

Now I was mobile. I was allowed to ride to school and I could go to meet my friends. I didn't wear jeans; they weren't yet in fashion so I struggled with a skirt which got in the way. I cycled for miles—got a few punctures, and learned to repair them—and learned to ride 'no hands' racing down hills. I remember the exhilarating feeling of wind rushing through my hair, burning my cheeks and filling my lungs.

The fifties was an era of great American musicals—Guys and Dolls, The King and I, South Pacific. And not to forget Marilyn Monroe singing Diamonds are a Girl's Best Friend. But swinging around a lamp post and singing—like Gene Kelly—was the most addictive. It was happy fun, energetic, romantic and *gay*. Just right for a teenager. For me, 'Singing in the Rain,' outshone all the others, it has been described as the greatest musical ever made. There were plenty vying to be the greatest.

The teens of the fifties listened to the 'Top 20' tunes each week on the latest portable radios; or in little kiosks in music shops. We bought 78 rpm records and played them on gramophones with needles which had to be carefully placed into a groove on the record. Lewis's, in Birmingham, had a large department in the basement where the top 20 were played over a loud speaker.

Dozens of new songs flooded the market—*Bewitched, Bothered and Bewildered–Goodnight Irene–My Secret Love–Little Things Mean a Lot–Memories Are Made Of This–Love Letters In The Sand–Be my Love.*

After we tried the records in Lewis's, we sometimes went to the Kardomah Cafe in New Street opposite the Burlington Arcade. It was a popular meeting place in 50s and 60s where we could treat ourselves to coffee and a Kunzle cake—if we could afford it. Kunzle Cakes were a treat to die for. 'Showboats' were thick chocolate shells, filled with sponge and decorated with cream and chocolate or sweets. Each was individually wrapped in cellophane. Kunzle's bakery was started in Fiveways Birmingham by a Swiss chef, Christian Kunzle. The firm was taken over in the 1960s. Today, Tesco's have an online recipe for making them.

In the 50s all the girls wanted to look like Doris Day who was singing, 'I'll see you in my dreams'. We copied her clothes. There were new colourful fashions that were cheap to buy or easy to make. Full skirted dresses with nipped in waists, pencil slim skirts with slits at the back, figure hugging dresses, patterned dirndl skirts, circular skirts and waspie belts to nip the waist even tighter. And when Dior introduced the pretty Princess Line, I made one in a lovely green colour. My friend was wearing baby doll dresses that were daringly shorter than ever. Just about every style was in fashion at the same time and we tried them all.

We wore our cardigans back to front and buttoned down the back— why I have no idea. Dolman sleeves and batwing sweaters were in fashion.

A new creaseless material, called Terylene, meant that pleated skirts never creased or lost the sharp pleats. Later women were wearing 'boxy' jackets with twin sets and pearls, and queuing for days in the crazy sales rushes that hit the fifties. Outlandish bouffant and beehive hairstyles appeared, achieved by back combing and curlers and we all wore Alice bands in our hair.

Peep toes, stilettos and winkle pickers with pointed toes, were fashion shoes of the fifties. The metal tips of stilettos, ruined many floors and also my parent's new dining table as I stood on it to have the hem of my wedding dress adjusted.

Teenage boys wore blazers and flannels and often suede shoes, jeans weren't the fashion. Around this time, electric razors began to take over from the 'cut throat razor'. Many of our friends were called up to do National Service or 'square bashing'. From 1945–1963, the Government called up two 2.5 million young men for Service

Teddy Boys arrived on the scene in 1952 in London East End. They wore knee length jackets that were close fitting, with narrow velvet lapels and cuffs; and waistcoats and shoestring ties. Trousers were narrow 'drainpipes' and crepe soled suede shoes or creepers for jiving, finished the look. The overall look was long and narrow and called the 'drape'. Teddy boys formed gangs which could be threatening, they were making their mark—as were all the new teenagers after the war.

The 1950s was the age of television. At first there was only one BBC channel which was black and white. Many sets were bought for the Coronation in 1953 but by the end of the decade most homes had one. It was the same for telephones which were acquired during those years.

The mystery of the 'abominable snowman' or the 'Yeti' from the mountain ranges of Tibet was topical conversation in the 1950's. Sir Edmund Hillary had conquered Mount Everest in 1953, and during one of his climbs saw huge mysterious footprints. The local Sherpa people had many legends about strange creatures, which seemed to be half ape and half man, which roamed the mountains. In 1960, Hillary mounted an expedition to try to find them. It seems a mystical creature does exist and through DNA testing of bones, is believed to be a cross between a polar bear and a brown bear.

The 50s was also the decade of the car. At the beginning there were few cars on the road, by the end most families owned one. Because of the increase of traffic on the road, the first zebra or pedestrian crossings appeared in 1949. In 1953 it became legal to wear seat belts and the first motorway, the M1, was opened in 1959.

Dad bought a car but it is his second car I remember most. It had the number plate WOB 234. The number indicated the simple way cars were registered in those days when so few were on the road. Later, when I was married, we had the treasured WOB 234, I wish we had kept the number plate.

One minute we were being very grown-up and the next behaving like kids, but I don't think we used the word *kids* in those days.

Maggie asked me, 'We're going up the tunnel this afternoon, want to come?'

'The tunnel, where's that?' I'd never heard it mentioned before, 'who is going?'

'Down the village near the allotments.' Maggie looked mysterious, 'the boys found it, but you mustn't tell.'

The boys were some of the youth club crowd. But that afternoon it would be four of the girls on an expedition 'up the tunnel.' It sounded fun and just right for teens who wanted a dare.

'Bring some food for a picnic and a torch,' said Maggie, 'and don't forget—don't say anything.'

I can't remember where the entrance was, but it was on some open ground—somewhere near Moor Pool estate in Harborne. It was a huge clay pipe, about four foot in diameter with four inches of water in the bottom pouring out into a drain.

'We can't go up there, look at the water.' It looked dark and wet.

'Yes we can. . .you have to put your feet either side of the water and bunny jump in, we've been before and there is a cave half way, but you can't turn round until you get there.'

We set off, torches in mouths, bunny jumping carefully because of the water; not able to raise our heads because of the height. At long last we reached the cave. It was a square section with four pillars for seats in each corner, just made for a teenage adventure picnic. Overhead was a manhole cover. We had our picnic in the cave, our voices made echoey noises with all the shrieks and laughter. It was cold and we didn't know if it was still light outside, and it wasn't much fun either. But it was a dare we had achieved and a story to tell. We made our careful journey back, I was relieved to stand up again.

'Where have you been all afternoon?' Mum asked.

'Up the tunnel, but I'm not supposed to tell you.' Alarm bells rang for Mum.

I explained and she nearly exploded, 'But that's a sewer and it's dangerous, if not a sewer an overflow pipe for the stream.'

She was right, probably a culvert under the road for a stream—but what if there was heavy rain and a flash flood whilst we were in there? What if someone opened the manhole in the road above and tipped something down? What if one of us had a panic attack and got stuck?. . .no-one knew we were there. But it was one of the list of things to do you before you die!

In 1951, Mum and Dad took Ann and me to the Festival of Britain in London. Mary by now was working so didn't come. I was so excited at the thought of going to London as well as to the exhibition. We walked around the exhibits and looked at the sculptures but my outstanding memory is of the incredibly high water sculpture made of 'buckets.' As the top-most buckets filled with water they overbalanced and then tipped over to fill those below and so on down through ten levels, to the fountain base. Each time a massive bucket tipped over, gallons of water splashed down to the next level, eventually crashing out in a foam at the bottom. The water sparkled in the sunlight. We watched fascinated for ages. It was a very hot day with clear blue skies and we wanted to jump in and swim in the crashing water.

The amazing 'Dome of Discovery' stood ninety-three feet tall and had galleries on various levels housing exhibitions on the Living World, the Polar world, the Sea, the Earth, the Physical World, the Land, Sky and Outer Space and a Planetarium.

The Festival was opened on the 3 May, 1951, by the King on the South Bank Site of the River Thames in London. It was to mark the centenary of The Great Exhibition of 1851.

The aim of the festival was to celebrate Britain's history, achievements, industry, science, the arts and culture. An event to help Britons forget the trauma of war and contribute to the post-war 're-construction' of morale. It was referred to as a *tonic to the nation.* There were over 10 million paid admissions in five months.

A year after opening the exhibition, the King died in his sleep at Sandringham on Wednesday 6 February, 1952. He was fifty-six and had suffered with cancer of the lung for some time.

The House of Commons was suspended as a mark of respect and all cinemas and theatres closed. BBC programmes were cancelled except for news bulletins. Flags in every town were at half-mast. The American President summoned the feelings in his tribute from the White House.

'The King shared to the end of his reign all the hardships and austerities which evil days imposed on the brave British people. In return, he received from the people of the whole Commonwealth, a love and devotion which went beyond the usual relationship of a King and his subjects.'. . .President Truman.

Princess Elizabeth was four thousand miles away in Kenya. When she returned she was Queen Elizabeth II. A new era had dawned. Elizabeth was crowned Queen on Tuesday 2 June, 1953 in Westminster Abbey. This was a huge responsibility for a twenty-five-year-old young wife and mother. At the Queen's insistence the whole event was televised by the BBC. Norman Hartnell, designed her white silk dress which was embroidered with the floral emblems of the countries of the Commonwealth.

We watched the Coronation on a neighbour's television, hung bunting from our windows and there were street parties throughout the land.

The Queen was driven from Buckingham Palace to Westminster Abbey in the Gold State Coach. She made her Coronation oath and was crowned with the gold Imperial crown by the Archbishop of Canterbury. He gave her the Orb, also made of gold and encrusted with many precious jewels and topped with a cross. The Orb represents the Monarch's role as Defender of the Faith. The Archbishop then gave her the Coronation Ring—'The Wedding Ring of England'. She wore it on the fourth finger of her right hand in accordance with tradition.

The return route to Buckingham Palace, was designed so that the Queen and her procession, could be seen by as many people in London as possible. The procession stretched for more than a mile. Those on foot marched ten abreast, whilst those on horseback were six abreast.

The Queen appeared with her family on the balcony of the palace still wearing the Imperial State Crown and the Royal Robes to greet the cheering crowds. She appeared again at 9.45pm, to turn on the 'lights of London'. Lights cascaded down the Mall from the Palace, to Admiralty Arch and turned the fountains in Trafalgar Square into liquid silver. Then all the floodlights from the National Gallery to the Tower of London were illuminated.

Who remembers Coronation Chicken? It was invented for the foreign guests who were entertained to lunch after the Coronation. The food had to be prepared in advance, and Constance Spry, suggested cold chicken in a curry cream sauce, with a salad of rice and green peas. In 1953, Constance Spry was still preparing debutantes for presentation to the Queen—the era of debutantes 'Coming Out' ended in 1958.

Teddy Boys thought of themselves as the new 'Edwardians,' *but we knew we were the 'New Elizabethans.'*

30

O DEAR ... O LEVELS

By the time we were in the upper fifth, we no longer ran in the corridors, ate in the street, or could avoid being caught. We conducted ourselves with decorum and propriety! The Front Entrance Hall was no longer forbidden territory. I crossed it one day and to my utter, (really, really utter) astonishment, saw a group of fourth year girls playing off ground touch on the seats outside the Head's office—'that sacred, never to be entered place without permission and then only on tiptoe and in silence.'—They stood on the seats and jumped or ran trying to catch each other. Sent there by an exasperated teacher, they seemed totally unconcerned about being caught.

They seemed to be enjoying themselves. I enjoyed school but there are some memories that make me wince. My school work was sadly suffering because of my social life. I dropped in class as my attention changed. Homework was done on the bus on the way to school. I forgot or lost anything and everything, that could be forgotten or detached. I lived in a dream world, only broken by a fear of school reports and the repeated comments—could do better. I knew I could, I must have absorbed and learned much by default rather than by intention.

And then, my life began to catch up with me. In November 1952, I stood in the entrance hall and waited to see the Headmistress who was checking reports. I hadn't expected this. We were due to take the new GCE exams June 1953; she needed to check that we were up to standard. I hadn't done well in the mock exams but was unperturbed—after all I had not studied, I thought I had lots of time.

The Head had other ideas. 'I have been reading your reports—your teachers say you could have done better.' I knew she was right. 'You have wasted some good opportunities.'

I just stood there—again she was right, I remembered my first year when I worked so hard.

'How many exams shall I enter you for?'

'Six.' That was the maximum allowed in the first trial years of O levels. I knew I could pass them if I studied, after all there was plenty of time.

She looked at me askance and sighed, 'I don't expect you will pass all of them but I will enter you.' Dismissively she said, 'You may go.'

So I went. But how did she know me? I felt sick in the pit of my stomach and I remember the feeling of exposure. I thought no one knew me or noticed me. I had never really been told off for anything. *And I had never played 'off ground touch' in the entrance Hall.* How could this be? Her words had the effect of challenging my stubbornness—I will show her I thought.

I went home, found a roll of wall paper and made a chart on the back, it filled my bedroom wall. I divided up every subject from the first year and worked out how much time I needed to catch up. The full horror hit me! I needed to work at least six hours every day, on top of school and homework in order to catch up. But I was going to do it even if only to prove myself to Miss D. who hadn't noticed me before.

With the usual excesses of youth, I was up at 5am the next morning; and the next from then on, and every evening until after midnight. I kept shouting, 'Be quiet, I'm trying to study.' My parents were not used to this. It must have been awful for them. I dropped every single social occasion for six months, day and night. Little by little I began to catch up. But it was strange because my knowledge was a year or so behind the class. They were studying fourth year work; I was becoming knowledgeable about the first year! My next report was grudgingly good but with, 'What a pity she hasn't worked like this before.'

I began to enjoy class discussions. I got a kick from the surprise on a teacher's face when she put a good mark on my work. It was a warm Spring and I remember studying for exams outside on the grassy banks of our lovely school. *I wished I had worked like this before. Dad was so right—'You will regret not working.'*

For once, I wasn't nervous about the exams when they came. I wasn't afraid as I waited in that hall for the results to be pinned on a board. I passed all the exams I took and I was grateful to the Headmistress who told me off—just in time. But would I have taken note if someone had said something before?

Leaving day came and I remember the sadness as I shared assembly and speech day for the last time.

For the last time we sang 'I vow to thee my country. . .entire and whole and perfect, the service of my love.

For the last time I watched the Head Girl spring to the platform to shout, 'Three cheers for Miss D.'

And then, 'Three cheers for the school.' The 'hip hip' and the rousing 'hooray,' that closed my school years brought tears to my eyes. I really had enjoyed school ... even when not working!

For the last time I walked out of the front entrance and down the drive. It was summer 1953. School days were over; exams were behind me. I was free and life was full of excitement and promise. But first we were going on another holiday to Dunster. What a privilege to be a teenager in the fifties.

31

DUNSTER BEACH IN THE 1950s

'Faster than fairies, faster than witches,
Bridges and houses, hedges and ditches;
Charging along like troops in a battle,
All through the meadows, the horses and cattle.
And ever again, in the wink of an eye,
Painted stations whistle by.'

Robert Louis Stevenson's, 'From a Railway Carriage,' sums up perfectly the mounting excitement and the flashing sights from the train that was speeding us to our home by the sea. The miles flew by, Exmoor rolled away, a patchwork counterpane of green hills and purple heather. . .bringing back memories of wild ponies, Lorna Doone, cream teas and *Dunster again*.

Finally, the big iron monster puffed and chugged its way into Dunster Station. Hissing steam, it pulled to a stop with a shrill whistle. We had arrived. Drifts of pink rosebay willow herb, scattered seeds along the track; and a kaleidoscope of thistles and wild roses clambered over the banks. I remember so clearly the wild flowers of Dunster.

The tiny empty station in the middle of nowhere, sprang to life as the train halted. The new arrivals for the beach for the next week, piled off the train and crowded excitedly and impatiently through the gate. A queue formed to collect trunks from the Station Master. I can't remember how we got our huge trunk from the station to the beach, perhaps it was a taxi.

The trunk—bought for emigration to Australia—was in good use. Mum had been packing it for weeks, clothes, sheets, books, dried foods, packet foods, tea, flour and sugar. Limited shopping only on Dunster beach. The trunk contained most of our family's needs for two glorious weeks.

It was fairly normal in those days to take a trunk on a family holiday. It was packed in advance and delivered to the station a few days beforehand; and then dispatched by the station for collection at destination.

We walked the lane to the beach. I remember hogweed that stood like tall sentinels, and blackberries that drooped heavy from hedges. Each year it was the same, blackberry time meant summer holidays were here. We picked the berries and the purple juice stained our lips and hands.

A few more yards and we saw the beach, would the tide be in? The sea sometimes seemed a mile away across patchy sand and pebbles when the tide was out. We had arrived. Our chalet was right on the beach, with doors that opened onto sand. Number 39, was really just a big shed. It was ten foot by sixteen foot and contained beds, chairs, table, deck chairs and a couple of cupboards but no running water or toilets. But it was heaps better than camping.

'How about a cup of tea,' said Dad, 'I'll go and fetch some water.' He was always ready for a cup of tea.

'Give me a hand unpacking the trunk,' Mum already had it open, 'It won't take long if we do it together.'

'The chip van comes tonight; can we have some?'

'Yes, that'll be easy for tea.'

At last we were installed and ready for the holiday.

Next day I woke in my strange bed, tingling with excitement as I remembered where I was. Out from the covers, onto scrubbed wooden boards, throwing open the doors, we were off. We ran and ran, feet sinking into cool soft sand. We ran towards the distant sea under a cloudless sky. The wind chased the clouds, blew our hair and filled our lungs with invigorating ozone. We raced and chased and dipped and dived and screamed like the wild birds soaring over the white tipped waves. The birds didn't seem to mind.

Mum smiled indulgently and busied herself tidying her little seaside home. This was bliss. 'We'll have bacon for breakfast.' The delicious smell was soon wafting over the sand—and will there be fried bread?

Dad said as usual, 'I'll make a nice cup of tea.' That was bliss.

Dad's brother arrived with our cousins and settled into a nearby chalet and then more friends and family joined us. It must have rained some days but I mostly remember days of sunshine and warm evenings when folk gathered in the dusk to chat in small groups. The long day ended with the moon riding high in clear skies of a myriad stars— well in my memory it always seemed clear. Low conversations and laughter punctuated the air. Light flickered as cigarettes were lit. . .legs stretched out. . .blankets were fetched as evening cool set in. Bedtime?—not for hours, we were on holiday. Old stories were retold, laughter fun and sleepiness.

Dad said, 'We'll walk into Dunster tomorrow.'

'And can we climb Grabbist again?' That big hill, with the fascinating hill fort and the 'Giant's chair,' drew us like magnets.

'Yes, if it's fine.'

'I'll stay behind to make lunch.' Mum fancied a morning in the deck chair reading her new book. 'And if you pick some whorts, I'll put them in an apple-pie.'

Whorts or whortleberries grow wild on Exmoor and are really wild bilberries. And so we climbed the hill and picked them, scratching our hands as we searched under the scrubby plants for the delicious free fruit. And then into Dunster for an ice-cream. Now Dad felt he was on holiday. After the brick buildings of Birmingham, the thatched cottages and cobbled streets of Dunster enchanted us. We loved the ancient Yarn Market and the Castle that towered over the village and could be seen for miles. It was a long walk back to the beach; we flopped onto the sand exhausted.

And finally to bed. On a calm night, when the tide was in, we listened to the sound of the waves lapping gently, persistently, lulling us to sleep. Sometimes the weather did change. We lay in our cosy beds listening to the sound of the rain on the roof, feeling safe as the wind whirled around the chalets, spinning the sand in the alleyways between. Sometime the wind whipped the waves and they pounded the shore crashing and lifting pebbles but we were safe inside.

'I'm glad I'm not in that marquee, the one that fell over,' reminisced Dad, thinking about the holiday in Pendine, 'That pole would have crashed right onto me.'

When we walked into Dunster, we stopped to talk to Tim on the way.

Tim lived in a shack he had built by the side of the lane. It looked to be a jumble of old blankets, over piles of stones and rough timber.

One day he said, 'Would you like to see inside?'

We already knew he could be trusted, 'Yes please, we'd like to.'

What a palace inside! It had two rooms, one was a sitting room with a comfy old chair, a working fireplace, a mantelpiece with a clock and lots of books. There was a bedroom too, with a bed and another heap of clothes.

The shack was in sight of Dunster Castle and Lady Luttrell kept a watchful eye on Tim's welfare. She sent supplies from time to time and the Station Master's wife checked on him regularly. Tim was friendly, scruffy and entirely harmless; but he was also an educated man and sometimes, for special occasions, he put on a smart suit with a waistcoat and tie.

Too soon the holiday was over but this time I wasn't going back to school. Sometime in my last year at Kings Norton, I applied to train as a nurse. After an interview at Queen Elizabeth Hospital in Edgbaston, I was offered a place to train as a State Registered Nurse in May 1955. I had two years to fill in, although I would have preferred to stay on at school. But for most of us in those days, seven years after the war, it wasn't an option.

What to do? In the end I went as a Laboratory Technician to the Queen Elizabeth Medical School. I worked for a Medical Research Chemist who was researching the effect of smoking on cancer. There were many groups in the UK and USA doing similar research at that time. One job I had, was to ply a home-made smoking-machine with cigarettes. I watched as thick black tar dripped down into flasks from the lighted cigarettes and made up my mind, I would not smoke. The following year in 1954, smoking was officially established as a cause of lung cancer.

32

IN THE FOOTSTEPS OF FLORENCE

I was impatient to start nursing, two years seemed a long time to wait but then my plans changed unexpectedly.

Mary came home one day and surprised us, 'I've applied to train as a nurse and I've had an interview.'

'But where? you've never mentioned it before.'

'No but I've thought about it, I'm going to Dudley Road Hospital,' and then she said, 'I've been accepted to start straight away.'

In no time she was enrolled in the Training school. I was so envious. When she came home off duty, I listened as she talked about hospital life. She told me about the cadet nurses, who were seventeen and working on the wards but were too young to start training.

'I could do that.' I thought, 'why wait?' As soon as I was seventeen, I applied, had an interview and was accepted to start in September, it was 1954. It was six years after the start of the NHS.

I wrote and cancelled my training at the Queen Elizabeth. Matron was not amused and sent me a very disapproving letter asking to see me. She didn't think it right to cancel my training; even when I explained that I wanted to start straight away. She was quite caustic and said until I was eighteen, I would always be the most junior on the ward. It was a privilege, she said, to be offered a place at the QE. She even phoned my Mother and asked her to talk to me. She was right but I had made up my mind.

I was always inspired by stories of Florence Nightingale, the 'Lady with the

Lamp.' So I was thrilled to learn that Dudley Road was built in 1889, on a design recommended by the great Florence herself.

I couldn't wait to go there. I gave in my notice and one afternoon, in September, I found myself at the hospital with a group of girls also hoping to be nurses. We were welcomed by one of the Sister Tutors, who inspired us with an introduction to nursing. She talked about Anne Gibson, the first Matron, who was a Nightingale nurse and set up the Nurse Training school.

'Nursing', she said, 'is a vocation and not a job,' and explained the priority it would have over our lives. 'You will be working long hours and need proper rest,' she reminded us. 'So you will live in the nurses' home and you must be in by 10pm when the door will be locked.'

Some girls exchanged looks. Most of us were used to later nights than that. We sat in silence as she continued.

'You need your sleep because you will work six days a week, from eight in the morning until eight at night, with three hours off during the day.' It sounded grim. 'But there will be one day off a week and one evening from five o'clock.' That worked out at 54 hours a week but included beaks.

'What about weekends?' someone asked.

'If you have a weekend off, you will need to work for twelve days in a row and your ward sister will work that out.' I was later to learn myself how difficult it was to work out shifts for a ward, making sure everyone had time off and yet the ward had enough staff cover.

We learned that we would not be paid a salary but would receive board and lodging and 'pocket money.' 'You are students in training and if you were at College or University, you would not receive anything, so you are lucky.'

Sister went on to explain about uniform. . .Hair was to be drawn back neatly under caps which must always be spotlessly clean. White aprons must always be clean. Black stockings with seams and black sensible shoes were to be worn—please keep spare stockings handy in case of ladders. Jewellery must not be worn under any circumstances and certainly no earrings or engagement rings. Wedding rings were permitted. No make-up on duty.

One girl asked about lipstick. 'Not even a trace, said Sister, why would you want to wear lipstick to nurse patients?'

She continued to explain, the nurses cloak, black with a red lining, must be worn around the hospital; never, ever wear cardigans over uniforms because of spreading infection. If we went out in our off duty, we must not wear our uniform with a coat over it. We must always change to full 'Mufti'—civilian clothes. A lecture on hygiene and the infection risk for committing these crimes followed.

Although the Sister Tutor was kind, we were all too scared to even think about breaking rules. I felt I was leaving the world and entering a convent, but I knew this was my vocation. Finally, she orientated us around the hospital and our accommodation. She left us to go for tea and settle into the home set aside for new trainees.

It was my first time away from home and I wanted to tell the family but there were no mobiles and I realised I really *was* leaving home; this was my family now. I was relieved when Mary dropped in with a group of friends.

'We thought we'd come and see the new girls,' they laughed at our apprehension, 'you'll soon get used to it.' We had lots of questions. Over the years, I learned how good it was to see Mary around the hospital. To share experiences or, 'Just hang out together,'—although that expression wasn't used then.

We found uniforms on our beds, we were to put them on for evening supper in the dining room and then for our first morning in school. The uniform for cadet nurses, was a white dress, apron and cap to distinguish us from nurses in training who wore blue dresses, white aprons and caps.

For six weeks we listened to lectures on; medicine, surgery, anatomy and every sort of patient hygiene—oral hygiene, bathing hygiene, bed-pan hygiene, hand washing hygiene and more hygiene for situations I didn't even know existed. By the time we got off duty, we just wanted to get into the bath.

We practised on a dummy how to bath a patient in bed, give the dummy an injection, how to give an enema and how to treat the dummy's pressure points.

'Nurses, it is a disgrace to have a bedsore,' We learned a bedsore must be reported to the highest level, to Matron, she who was to be feared.

'But Nurses it must *not* happen, it is sign of poor nursing, pressure points must be treated every day.'

It soon became an important part of our routine and we shared the fear of the disgrace that a bedsore would bring to the sister, the ward and to us. We made beds–learned how to carry and empty bedpans correctly–how to correctly put on a gown and gloves for sterile procedures–how to lay up sterile trolleys for procedures that left the mind boggling—did people really have that done to them?

We even learned how to apply leeches. We had a jar of live leeches and were told they were still used on the Mission Field. Back in the 1800s, blood-letting with leeches was a normal practice in England for almost any condition when it was thought too much blood caused disease. *But not now, why did we need to know this?*

'I want a volunteer,' said sister, 'to have one applied.'

Everyone shrank back in disgust. 'Ugh, no way.'

'Come on nurses, it doesn't hurt.'

Eventually someone agreed. We watched transfixed as Sister took a fat leech, looking a bit like a slug, from the jar and held it close to a small vein on her wrist. Mouths dropped as it clamped a suction-like mouth onto the vein. We watched as the leech started to swell with blood and in a few minutes dropped off—it was full!

'No, I didn't feel a thing.' said the brave nurse.

'That's because it applies an anaesthetic to the skin,' sister explained, 'as well as a substance that encourages bleeding.' This seemed ridiculous, we didn't bleed patients today–not today.

Needless to say we didn't use them on the wards in 1954. *But they are making a come-back today in the treatment of some circulatory disorders, their saliva contains an enzyme which helps blood flow freely—go online and check it out!*

The only 'blood letters' on the wards were the doctors who came to take blood for tests. Taking blood was quite an elaborate procedure. A syringe and needle was boiled in a sterilising tank on the ward and placed into a sterile receiver—also boiled—swabs for cleaning the vein were taken from a drum with sterile forceps. The whole was covered in a towel taken from a drum of sterile towels. Preparing a trolley for this procedure was the nurses' job. By the time I was a third year nurse, needles and syringes in neat disposable packs, came from a central sterile supply and nurses were allowed to take blood—that was progress.

And so we were prepared for any situation a junior nurse might encounter on the wards. We were 'processed.' Although I was a cadet nurse and would for the next nine months be at the bottom of the ladder, I learned every procedure too.

'Sister will watch you do all these procedures on the wards and when perfected, you will be marked in your ward book, don't think you are proficient yet.'

We especially learned about infection control and why the hospital was built on the design laid down by Florence Nightingale. A design that was still important in 1954.

In the days before antibiotics, Florence taught that good nursing for recovery, meant fresh air, light, warmth, cleanliness, quiet, and a good diet. *Quite simply . . .good nursing and the prevention of cross infection from one patient to another.*

Dudley Road was built on her recommended design with all of this in mind. It comprised a single corridor, stretching like a spine, for a quarter of a mile, with separate blocks of wards radiating alternately from either side. The separation of blocks, was intended to minimize cross infection and aid ventilation and sunlight. The corridors between, were open to the elements for the same reason. Dudley Road corridor is famous for being the longest hospital corridor in the country and is the symbol on the hospital badge. The long wards had tall windows at regular intervals on either side, again for good ventilation, with space between each window for a single bed. The end of each ward had an open section of four beds for 'open air' infectious nursing. Extensive gardens surrounded the wards to aid psychological recovery.

The hospital had not changed from its early design when I started nursing. Today it has grown considerably and those open corridors are closed in. The Front Tower, entrance and Porters Lodge were demolished in 1964 for a new A&E.

33

MY FIRST WARD

Six weeks later, after initial training in school, I nervously reported for duty at 8am to C11, a female medical ward on the second floor. Sister was small, her blonde hair tucked under her frilly sister's cap and wearing a navy uniform with long sleeves and frilly cuffs. She looked sternly at me as if summing me up. Her first words were 'Stand here and listen to the night nurse's report.'

I stood in the glass windowed office, with the other nurses reporting for day duty and listened; but it didn't mean much to me that morning. I looked down the old fashioned ward which had rows of beds on either side. There were forty beds, with white counterpanes and bedside lockers. The patients' names and temperature charts hung on the wall behind the bed. Here and there was an oxygen tent over a bed, where a patient had breathing difficulties. There were no curtains to screen the beds in those days. Screens were mobile and pulled into place when required.

My attention had wandered and I realised duties were being allotted. I found I was to work with a senior nurse and to start making the beds with her. The linen trolley had been loaded ready for us by the night staff and was piled high with fresh white linen of every description. I pushed it to the first bed and fetched the dirty linen bin and we started to work our way down one side of the ward.

Here at least I knew what I was doing. During our few weeks in school we had made beds 'correctly' many times. I could do the 'envelope' corners, change a draw-sheet under a patient whilst protecting their modesty. I could fix the back rests, make a patient comfortable and knew how to lift a patient correctly. I relaxed, taking my cue from the senior nurse, as we chatted to the always grateful patients. Suddenly the nurse speeded up. She nodded to the other side of the ward. The ward sister, who had completed her early round of checking the patients, had rolled up her sleeves and was making beds with another nurse. There was a light-hearted competitiveness about it.

The morning chore of making the beds soon became a favourite occupation as well as a time to get to know the patients. There was a sense of pride in seeing the freshly made beds and the comfortable patients.

Sister would then stand at the end of the ward and survey the beds. 'Straighten those wheels.' she would say, pointing to bed wheels that were out of alignment. She was a stickler for neatness as well as patient comfort.

All the nurses cared for all the patients in those days. Patients were not allotted to specific nurses, 'that's not my patient' was never heard. I soon learned the Sister on C11 would do any job on the ward, however menial, if necessary. She was strict but very good and the nurses respected her. It was rumoured that she had once been a 'Bluebell Girl', dancing with a high-kicking dance troupe, at the Folies-Bergère in the 1940s in Paris. The last remaining company to dance the traditional 'can-can', performing in glittering clouds of sequins, ostrich feathers, voluminous headgear and not a great deal else. For various reasons I came to believe it might be true as time went on, although she never discussed her private life.

There were usually five nurses on duty for the busy start of the day. This was when the heaviest work on the ward was done. Beds were made and the ward cleaned and tidied. For the rest of the day there would be two or three nurses plus Sister or Staff Nurse in charge.

Four or five nurses looking after forty patients, meant that we were always busy—bed making, bed baths, medicines, dressings, recording temperatures, preparing patients for theatre, admitting patients, discharging patients, testing urine and much more than can be listed here. Then there was the ward round when the consultant or senior doctor, expected up to date information and test results.

The junior nurse gave out bedpans, cleaned the bedpans, cleaned the sluice, cleaned the trolleys, cleaned the lockers, cleaned the beds of discharged patients, cleaned patients' teeth and gave out even more bedpans. As I was always the junior nurse for the next year, I spent my time cleaning. Matron at the Queen Elizabeth hospital was right. . .but I was happy.

For my first evening on duty, a Senior Nurse was in charge.

At around 7pm she said, 'Go to the ward entrance and watch for the Asmats.' I wondered if she was joking but then, 'Shout Asmats when you see them.'

I looked at her with disbelief. 'What on earth are Asmats?' I imagined some sort of alien or a darlek-like creature trundling down the corridor.

She laughed. 'Asmats,' she explained, 'are Assistant Matrons who do the ward rounds in the evening, we need to know when they are coming.' Of course it was so obvious! Those Asmats read all the ward reports and knew everything about every patient; they questioned the nurse in charge about treatment, drugs etc.

A few days later I was on another evening shift. A junior nurse, just ahead of me, was on the same ward. We seemed to finish the work early that night. So she said 'Come into the bathroom and take the weight off your feet.' I was ready for a break.

She flopped herself down into the bath, her long legs dangling over the side sighing 'This is so comfortable, come and join me.'

I did just that. I dropped into the bath and I was just saying, 'This isn't comfortable,' when quick as lightening, she jumped out and turned the taps full on.

'Now you've been initiated,' she said laughing hilariously at the sight of me. I don't know how I got off duty with a wet uniform.

As the perpetual junior nurse on the ward, I often got the 'off duty' no one wanted. This usually meant working from 8–9.30am and then having the morning off until 12.30pm. After lunch it was back on the ward to work through until 8pm at night. It was a long day and how my feet ached. It was all I could do to have supper in the nurses dining room and then flop onto my bed unable to move. Sometimes I awoke stiffly in the early hours, still in my uniform, I had been so tired. How did anyone survive this and have the strength to go out socialising at the end of the day? It was all work it seemed at the start.

Somehow I did gain strength and supper-time in the dining room, recounting the day's stories became a highlight. I was close friends with four other nurses and when we were off duty together, we would collapse in the Nurses' Home; telling stories and giggling for ages over the most trivial things.

Wendy had a real sense of humour and could be relied on to make us laugh. She was clever and when the time came was awarded the first prize in our final exams. Sally was petite, dark haired and quiet. She worked as a Nanny for a family on a farm in Shropshire before starting her training. Sometimes I went with her to the farm for a weekend whilst the farmer and his wife took time off. I was amazed at how competent she was in running the household. Probably why she was such a competent nurse.

Patsy was blonde and pretty with a bit of a giggle and the first of our set to wear what seemed outrageously short 'baby-doll' dresses. She had the figure to carry it off and in fact was often first to try a new fashion. We were all so different. When the rest of us forgot or lost things Alice could always be relied on to supply anything from a safety pin to a needed cup of tea. She did the most superb needlework and embroidery, often making presents for her friends. We did PTS together and had years of fun. *Their names have been* changed their names to protect anonymity.

The Nurses' Home was an attractive building, surrounded by extensive gardens and within the hospital complex. We had our own rooms but the bathrooms were shared. Whatever the age, eighteen or 21, it was still lights out at 10pm. The night Sister did regular rounds and knocked if she saw a light under a door. Many times we sat late and chatted with friends, turning off the light and going silent as we heard her coming. We held our breath, as she hovered by the door listening for whispers, before moving on.

If caught in the bathroom after 10pm there would be a knock on the door, 'Hurry up nurse, you should be in bed.'

In many ways, living in the home in the hospital grounds, we were cut off from the outside world. There was a pay-phone but it was rarely used except for planned calls. If we needed to contact someone, we wrote letters in the same way as we write emails. Mum and Dad were brilliant and both wrote every week—separately—they knew we wanted to hear from them. Response to a letter was quick, usually the next day by return post.

I collected one letter from Mum from my pigeon hole in the dining room and sat down to read it. I pulled out several connected sheets of Izal toilet paper.

'What on earth is that,' said a friend.

'A letter from Mum, she says she ran out of writing paper.' We all laughed.

The sheets were closely covered in writing. Mum always did have a sense of humour—she knew that sort of thing would lighten our day. Izal toilet paper was like thin greaseproof paper, on a roll with perforated sheets.

Dad was very proud of Mary and me although he often joked about us being involved in the slave trade. During the Suez Crisis when petrol was strictly rationed, Dad saved up petrol so that he always had enough to take us back to hospital after days off.

After two months on C11, the Staff Nurse told Sister that I had not yet seen a dead patient and that I was scared. Sister sent for me.

'You will help lay out the next patient that dies and this time don't run off into the sluice.'

The sluice, as the most junior of juniors, was my domain and a good hiding place.

'Yes Sister.'—I don't know why I was so anxious. There had never been a death in our family; perhaps I subconsciously related it to some experience during the Blitz.

C11 was a female ward with chronic long term medical illnesses. The patients were often on the wards for several weeks and there was a high mortality rate from heart and lung diseases. A good number came in with pneumonia and many died. C11 was on the top floor, and the jingle went, '*C11 the ward nearest heaven,*' because of the number of deaths during the winter months.

Before long there was a death on the ward. I had got to know this patient well over the weeks as I made her bed and attended to her generally. On the morning she died, I had chatted to her. I was summoned to the office and when Sister told me, I could feel tension rising.

She said—quite kindly, 'You will go with Staff Nurse,' and I was taken behind the screens that were round the bed.

I looked at the patient and stared. 'But she's not dead.' She *was* dead but she didn't look any different, she just wasn't responding. And so my fear was broken, after that I coped with laying out the dead but it was never a job I felt happy doing.

At the end of my first month I went to collect my pay from the Bursar. We were paid in cash, and I checked the amount. For my long month of work, I had earned £5.19s.6d. But as we were often told it wasn't pay, it was an allowance of pocket money. We were student nurses and as students, shouldn't get paid. We were told we were lucky; this allowance had been negotiated—not without difficulty! However, it was often said that a hospital could not function without the labour of student nurses. Uni. students may not get an allowance but they did not work as we did. Nevertheless, I rarely heard a complaint from student nurses about pay— after all this was our vocation.

34

AT LAST I CARRY A LAMP

It was not all hard work, there were amazing times of fun and friendship. I will never forget Christmas in Hospital and especially my first one in 1954. All the wards were decorated with different themes and preparations were secretly made for weeks in advance, each ward trying to outdo the others. The sister on C11, if not a Bluebell Girl, had certainly been a dancer. A few weeks before Christmas, she called the ward staff together and told us she had chosen her theme. It was going to be the Dance of the Sugar Plum Fairy!

From then on, *in any spare time we had*, we were busy making pink net ballet skirts for the bed lights and superb wall posters appeared, depicting scenes from the ballet. The standard was very high as professional help was drawn from theatre friends. There were free standing cardboard cut outs of ballerinas, with pink or white net skirts to stand at the doorways. Sister had involved her relatives and got sponsorship from somewhere and also collected money for the celebrations. A few days before Christmas, a huge tree was delivered and put in place at the end of the ward. Naturally, it was decorated with dainty ballerinas in coloured net skirts and intertwined with fairy lights.

Over the weeks up to Christmas, we were given endless boxes of chocolates from patients and bottles of drinks of all sorts. These were stored away in ward cupboards. A Christmas cake was made and iced with—ballerinas of course. For the only time in the year, we would be allowed to eat on the wards and the side ward was prepared with tables for food. Christmas crackers were made for the patients and decorated with ballerinas. Tiny presents were put inside. For staff presents, we had a 'lucky dip.' Each nurse bought one present up to 5s in value, and these were buried in box of sand, with ribbons attached.

The day came when we attached the net skirts to the lights, which were big old fashioned white glass globes, over each bed. The pink skirts hung gracefully over the lights and when the lights went on there were lots of, 'ohhhh how lovely.' This was a female ward so the feminine touches were appreciated. Again when the tree lights went on, the ballerinas twirled and sparkled in the warmth.

On Christmas Eve, many nurses took part in carol singing round the wards. We assembled at 9pm after day-duty. I was with my friends and waved excitedly to Mary, with a group of her friends. We turned our black cloaks inside out, wearing the red lining outside, and were given a lighted lamp to carry. We walked in pairs, the doctors joined the end of a very long 'crocodile' of nurses and we started off around the wards.

As we reached each ward the lights were turned off, apart from the tree lights. Then the procession, singing the old familiar carols, made its way the length of each ward; turned round the tree at the end and came back down the other side. The end of the 'crocodile' was still coming in, as the first were leaving, there were so many of us. Many tears were shed by patients, as they saw their red cloaked nurses singing as they carried their lanterns. That was always an unforgettable start to Christmas.

Every nurse had to be on duty for Christmas. There was a full complement of staff, and as many patients had gone home, the work was light and shared by everyone. We were allowed to go off the ward in turns, to visit friends and other wards visited ours. The doors regularly opened as nurses and sisters came to see friends, admire the decorations and chat to old patients they knew and have a glass of sherry. The doctors were on the ward and shared in the fun. On Christmas day the ward medical consultant, came in with his family, to carve the turkey.

Unofficially, we were allowed to eat on the wards but still had to make an appearance in the dining room. Unbelievably the meal that day was always stew and rice pudding! Boxing Day was a repeat of Christmas day, but also the day for the Nurses' Christmas Dinner. We took it in turns to go down to the dining room and it was always an excellent meal.

Eventually I was eighteen, put on a blue dress and repeated the six weeks PTS training. I had been a junior nurse on C11 for almost a year and most of the girls I started with were now in their second year. I sailed through PTS with my year experience and was looking forward to moving onto different wards. When told which ward to report to—I found I was back on C11. The ward sister had asked for me to go back; she had trained me for a year and wanted to take advantage of it. Nevertheless, this time it would only be for three months before I moved to another ward.

Nine months later, in midwinter, I was put on night duty for three months. Night duty meant working twelve hours a night straight through— for five nights a week. A sixty-hour week and it was really hard work but we had two nights off to compensate. There were two nurses on duty per ward. We started at 8pm listening to the day report. After that there was a mad rush to check each of forty patients–then to take round night-time drinks, medicines and bedpans. In between these routines, critically ill patients were checked and when we were 'on take,' emergencies were admitted.

At some point a night sister would arrive to check how we were doing. She asked questions about patients and we were expected to know the answer. The night continued to be busy even after lights out. At times a doctor was needed, or a patient died, or a bed needed to be changed.

At last I really became a Lady with a Lamp as I made regular checks around the sleeping ward—even if my lamp was a torch.

Sometimes, doctors came in for a chat and to scrounge food when they could.

One doctor particularly irritated us with. . .'I'd love a sandwich.'

One night we were prepared, and the sandwich was made. Cleaning soap was delivered to the ward in long yellow blocks. It looked like cheese. So much like cheese that when it was thinly sliced and put into a sandwich with tomato it looked delicious.

He took a huge, really huge bite—we thought his manners were atrocious anyway.

'Urghh, what on earth is this.' He was literally foaming at the mouth. 'This isn't cheese.'

'Oh, isn't it—sorry.' He didn't ask again. We didn't mind feeding some doctors who asked politely.

After a busy night we were often exhausted but at the unearthly hour of 5am, the lights were on again. It was far too early to wake patients with a cup of tea. It wouldn't happen now, the system is different, but we had masses of work to get through in the next three hours.

There were only *two nurses* but before 8am we had to make six beds, blanket bath two patients, treat pressure points, do a bedpan round, cook and serve the breakfast—yes we really did cook breakfast for forty patients—check the critically ill, do the drug round, load up the linen trolley for bed-making for the day staff, clean the sluice, take temperatures and make sure patients charts were up to date, answer the night sister's questions on her morning round—and finally write the night report, all before the day staff came on at 8am.

When I was on night duty in the summer, I used to sneak out onto the fire escape in the early morning, to breathe the fresh air and see the first glimmers of dawn. I often thought this was the best time of the day and yet no one sees it. The air is so cool and fresh and the first birds are beginning to sing. After a busy night there seemed an expectancy in the air of a new day. You could see for miles over the city and gardens from that top floor fire escape. I loved it too when I was on the district and called out on my bike in the early morning, or returning after a night-time delivery.

Holidays were a welcome relief. Mary and I went on one of the new package holidays to Italy. We planned it for months and one day, after we had both been on night duty, we flew to Rimini. The town in those days was little more than a large village with one long street and our pretty hotel. It was hot and sunny and everything we wanted, and our room had a balcony—bliss.

We were exhausted but, 'Shall we explore?'

'Yes let's, just a quick look.'

The beach was fabulous with clean white sand and a blue, blue sea.

One of us said, 'Let's sun-bathe'. We lay on the soft sand and within seconds fell asleep. We awoke sometime later to the sound of rustling and whispering. We couldn't believe our eyes.

'Go away.' We hastily tried to cover our exposed legs, burning in the sun, 'Go away.'

We were surrounded by a large circle of young Italians sitting shoulder to shoulder and staring at us and talking rapidly in Italian. We kept waving them away, they just laughed and stared but eventually moved back a few feet.

'Me, Arrigo,' said one, pointing to himself, 'You?'

We scrambled to collect our things and started back to the hotel, only to be followed by the group. Two of them came into the hotel with us and we learned they were the owners' sons.

It was out of season and there were so few visitors in town that the two English girls were front page news. We were already known everywhere we went, in the bank for money it was, 'You English girls.'

Everywhere — in the shops, walking by the sea, in the cafe's. After we got over the shock, we both went out on dates with Arrigo and his brother, they were very good looking. The brother asked Mary to stay on, but they were just holiday romances although the boys did write a few times after we returned.

One night, when I was on duty on one of the easier wards, the assistant matron came and asked me to go and help out in Summerfield Hospital. A nurse was off sick, leaving only one on duty on a large ward. My heart sank. I had been told how hard it was by other nurses who had been 'borrowed' to help out from time to time. For once I was on an easier ward and looking forward to a peaceful night.

Summerfield, built in 1848, was originally Birmingham Union Workhouse. At its peak it housed over two thousand inmates. Families came here who fell on hard times. They entered through the 'Arch of Tears,' where they were separated into separate gender and living groups. Divided families—husbands from wives—children from parents. So much heartache, so many tears, so much loss of hope. Eventually in 1948 under the NHS, the workhouse became Summerfield Hospital, a geriatric hospital and part of the Dudley Road Hospital group.

The call came at about 11pm. I clearly remember going down the metal fire escape on the ward, across the grounds and gardens surrounding DRH, through a gate in the Victorian red brick wall which divided the two hospitals, through a large entrance hall into a fine old building of elegant proportions.

Summerfield was no longer a workhouse, but I was shocked. The ward I was called to was a large geriatric male ward, of about one hundred beds—

twice the size of DRH wards. Although it was nearly midnight, the lights were full on. One male nurse was struggling, on his own, to change a wet bed.

'I've come to help, what do want me to do?'

'I'm afraid we'll spend most of our time, if not all our time, changing beds.' He was apologetic. 'It's a constant round—there's usually two of us.' Tonight he was on his own.

All night we changed wet and soiled beds and all night the lights stayed on. Many of these men had dementia, or were paralysed after a stroke, many were incontinent and had bed sores—not from neglect but from too few staff. The smell of the ward was awful and so was the noise from the men who were constantly shouting.

I really admired the nurse I was working with, he was totally dedicated to his job and willing to stay where no one wanted to work. It was labour of love. I felt guilty that I hadn't wanted to go to help.

It was so sad. These were old men, probably alone and unable to look after themselves. Many were terminally ill. I remembered how we transferred patients to Summerfield from DRH, when we couldn't discharge them home because of age and infirmity. They came here to die. It wasn't the workhouse but it was still a place of no hope for these elderly men.

It was 1955 and the NHS was only seven years old, and struggling to cope with healthcare for every need. There was nowhere for these men– or women– to go, except to what they still remembered as the 'workhouse.' It was tragic. *Those are old days that I wouldn't want back*

In February 1999, Dr Carl Chinn unveiled a commemorative plaque in what was known as the 'Arch of Tears' in the entrance to the old Birmingham Workhouse. . .later Summerfield Hospital.

'In memory of all those folk forced by hardships through the archway of tears and into the workhouse. In life they endured misfortune, in death they may rest in peace.'

The workhouse building was a stunning piece of Victorian architecture but is now derelict and with an uncertain future.

Back in Dudley Road, we had fun as well as hard work. There was always someone off-duty in the nurses' home to spend time with. It was like a big family and there was always somewhere to go. But even when we were nearly twenty-one, we still had to be back in hospital by 10pm. It seems there was a 'spy system' in place between the Porter's Lodge—which had to be passed—and the Nurses' home. If a Nurse came in late, I think the porter phoned the Home Sister to say a 'late nurse' was on the way. Somehow, Sister always knew when someone was coming.

Most of us developed social lives after we coped with the initial tiredness. Some of my Youth Club friends were now at Birmingham University and I went to the Union 'Hop' from time to time on a Saturday night. There were also the usual hospital romances, parties in the nurses' home and parties in the doctor' home—which was out of bounds to nurses. At Christmas the Doctors put on a show with sketches, poking fun at the Consultants or Senior Nurses. We all laughed at the 'in jokes' knowing the people they referred to.

Just before Christmas 1956, my friend Wendy went off sick with flu. After a busy day, I visited her on sick bay. . .the Christmas lights dazzled my eyes and blurred together.

I crashed down exhausted 'Are you feeling any better?'

'I can go home tomorrow.' She nodded and looked so comfortable in bed. 'But you look awful. . .have you got it now?

'No, definitely not.' I felt hot and the lights were so bright and my head was aching 'Just tired, we've been so busy.'

She didn't believe me, she called the sister who took my temperature; within minutes I was in the next bed. For once I was a patient. No wonder I ached and everything was blurred, my temperature was well over 100F.

Later the assistant matron did her round and with a twinkle in her eye, said 'It's those late nights at the doctor's parties, nurse.'

I was incensed but too slow and too weary to answer. . .I *was* going out with one of the doctors but had never been to a doctor's party. I kept the rules. I grumbled to my friend.

'Yes, but she probably knows who you are going out with.'

Yes, but I *still* hadn't been to the doctor's home. I was so annoyed. I also had a problem, we were going out to a Christmas party—how could I let him know I was off sick? There were no mobile phones and I couldn't go to a pay-phone. Somehow he found out and came to see me on sick bay. To make up for it took me to the Bell at Belbroughton for a meal. I had never been inside a pub before—that was not unusual in 1956 and not many pubs served food in those days. I loved the vintage atmosphere and I remember we had trout and I wore a 'bluebell blue' suit.

The years flew by and before long I was putting on second year cuffs and then my third year belt. These were used to identify the stage each nurse was at. At regular intervals we returned to training school to learn new procedures, and to study medicine and surgery at the appropriate level for the year. By the third year, I was often in charge of a ward when Sister and Staff Nurse were off duty. I thoroughly enjoyed the challenge as I developed my skills—I knew how to make a patient comfortable, did ward rounds with doctors, wasn't phased by emergencies and prided myself on my 'trolleys' for the many different procedures.

Things were changing rapidly in the NHS. At some time during these years we stopped boiling needles, syringes and instruments on the ward— blunting needles in the process—and a central supply delivered them. What a relief to have a disposable sterile pack containing one syringe, with a brand new sharp needle for each injection. The central supply posed new techniques to be learned, unpacking the sterile packs and 'laying up' trolleys without touching the contents. We learned.

But close to home and important to me, bedpan sterilisers arrived on some wards and the awful job of hand cleaning bedpans was over—the job I had done so long with pride. More new antibiotics were available to treat previously untreatable diseases. This meant that on some wards, the open air section was closed in to make patient lounges. On others, patients were still occasionally nursed in the open air. They weren't completely open, the sides and the top were closed in. It was open where four tall high windows would have been. It was cold in winter nursing patients out there, at least we were cold, the patients were warm. *Florence would be pleased at our fresh air attempts.*

The patients nursed on those wards were infectious, so we learned to 'barrier nurse' them. There were elaborate procedures with sterile gowns for nursing, for the correct disposal of soiled bed linen, careful hand washing— actually scrubbing to the elbow—the wearing of gloves and masks. I was reminded of this in the recent Ebola outbreak.

In the general part of the ward some patients were nursed for weeks and came in several times. We got to know them well, listened to family stories, sharing their fears, their sorrows and joys. Some stories and conditions were really harrowing and although we were taught to switch off, at times it was impossible. There was heartbreak and tragedy. . .The young mother who was dying and leaving toddlers. . .the strapping young man dying of leukaemia and us watching it happen. Real stories from real people.

Sometimes we wheeled a patient to the hospital chapel for a time of quiet. The chapel was a sanctuary of peace for nurses too who were struggling with life and death issues. It was open for nurses to meet together on Thursday evenings. Many found it a place to renew their own hope and strength. Facing the fragility of life and the certainty of death could not be avoided but our job was to comfort and care as well as we could. When I started nursing in 1954, some of the wards started the day with Sister leading prayers for patients and staff. A normal practice before the war which lingered on in many hospitals for several years.

As I completed my training, I worked on theatre, casualty, surgical wards, fracture wards and children's wards getting proficiency ticks in my ward book. Eventually, I took my final exams and qualified as a State Registered Nurse. I was so proud of my frilly cap and check dress that one morning I took a walk down the long corridor just to show it off to anyone I knew. I so thrilled. I was qualified after all this time.

One night, in my final months at DRH, I was invited to a BBQ in a country house belonging to one of the doctors. I had a late pass. We had an amazing time, swimming in the lake by the house and partying all evening. Lots of nurses and lots of doctors. Around 11pm, folk started to leave. As I had helped organise the event, I needed to stay and clear up. The house 'on loan' to us was not occupied and had to be left spotless. It was 3am before we finished—just four of us stayed, two doctors and two nurses. We arrived home as dawn broke and it was 4am. My late pass had expired. One of the doctors, just a friend, walked me down the drive to the home. I can't remember how I got in.

I was to be on duty at 8am, but before then I had phoned my mother to say what happened. I somehow guessed there would be trouble. I was apprehensive, even though I was twenty-one and now qualified. Matron was no longer 'in loco parentis' but remained vigilant. *It is a sign of a different time that we recognised those boundaries.*

As soon as I reported for duty on Theatre, Sister greeted me with, 'I am surprised at you Staff Nurse, you were seen walking to the Home at 4am with one of the doctors, I am surprised at him too,' she paused to let her words sink in, 'What do you think your mother would say?' I was so relieved that I could tell her my mother already knew, and explained we stayed to clear up after the other party goers.

'Well,' she said, 'Matron wants to see you immediately.'

My heart sank. Matron repeated the same as Sister and, 'What do you think your mother would say?' Again, I nervously answered that my Mother knew.

She stared at me and finally said, 'Don't let this happen again, go off duty now and get some sleep, you can't work on Theatre in that state.' I fled to my bed relieved. I guess I had earned enough 'brownie points' to stand me in good stead.

I can't remember what Mum said, she was probably sympathetic. But if I was living at home it would be, 'You treat this place like a hotel. . .and what do think the neighbours would think!' It was time for me to move on and be independent.

It was 1959. What an amazing decade it had been. During those years, Birmingham changed from identity cards and rationing, slums, barbed wire and derelict buildings, through change after change. Some good, some inadequate but necessary at the time. The City lost some beautiful Victorian treasures and built over four hundred blocks of high rise flats. Flats and prefabs, replaced many bomb damaged homes and back-to-back houses. Plans were made for the redevelopment of the Bull Ring and for ring roads and flyovers that changed the face of the City.

We lived through the Suez crisis which resulted in two years of petrol rationing, and then the Cold War with all its sinister threats. But the mini-car had arrived, televisions became the 'norm', many home installed telephones, fridges became commonplace as did package holidays. We had the Festival of Britain and the Coronation. In 1953, James Watson and Francis Crick deciphered the mysteries of DNA — the double helix containing the coded instructions of life. In 1957, the European Economic Community was established, and there was much more.

Fabulous fifties clothes and music arrived. Modern simple line of furniture appeared, bright pastel colours, chrome legged chairs, Formica tops and bold designs—now desirable retro, or vintage. Supermarkets began to appear, changing the way people shopped and Rackhams built a superb new store, a great place for the latest clothes, and a superb delicatessen with foreign foods. We tried Pizza for the first time! *It made me want to travel.*

35

CALL *THIS* MIDWIFE

In my last months at DRH, I met my future husband, a Research Student at Birmingham University. We planned to marry in 1961, after he completed his PhD degree, so I decided to train as a Midwife whilst waiting. This meant six months of study and experience in a Maternity hospital, followed by six months on the district under the supervision of an experienced midwife. I found that I thoroughly enjoyed midwifery. It was thrilling working with a mother through the months of waiting and then deliver a baby, hear the first cry and share the joy of the family.

I spent the first months at Hallam Maternity Hospital in West Bromwich and then moved to cover the district of Harborne. I was allowed to live at home—after it was explained to my mother that her nights would be disturbed by calls to me. She was great and took it in her stride. She agreed to answer the phone during the night if a call came when I was out. Many times she got out of bed to take a message, record it and got up again to pass it on when I returned. She was pleased to have me home and to share in my life again. Bless her.

And would I be allowed to use my Coventry Eagle Bike? No, I must use the black, 'bone shaking' sit up and beg supplied to midwives. A streamlined fast bike, did not quite suit the image of a district midwife.

I needed a bike with a basket to carry my black bag which contained the necessities for delivering a baby at home. Most important was a pack containing ligatures, forceps and scissors for cutting a new baby's cord. The pack had to be prepared and sterilised at home. After each birth, the instruments were cleaned, packed into a paper sack and sterilised in the domestic oven for one hour. A spare pack needed to be on hand at all times in case of emergencies.

The very week I started on the district, the Midwife on the next district, went off on long term sick leave. My supervising midwife agreed to cover both districts. As I was the only pupil, I also covered both districts. That meant twice as many clinics to run, twice as many mothers to support, twice as many homes to check for suitability, twice as many babies to deliver. From the very first day I was under double pressure. It seems there was an explosion of new babies. My Supervisor worked with me for the day work, but left me to the night work, once she checked that I was competent.

Only a small number of babies were delivered in hospital in the fifties, the rest were born at home. The district midwife taught mothers about child birth, nutrition, baby bathing and feeding. Prior to a birth, there was a home visit to ensure adequate preparations were in place and to explain the procedure to a mother and her 'helpers'—often her own mother or a neighbour.

On one home visit, the door was opened by the father who was blind. I discussed with mother the preparations and when I asked who was going to be her helper he said, 'I am.'

'But I will need hot water carrying upstairs. . .'

He laughed, 'No problem, watch me.' He filled a huge saucepan with hot water and carried it to the foot of the stairs. 'Look,' he said—I looked and there was not the slightest movement on the surface of the water. There were three pre-school children running around, he supervised them at the same time with an iron rod as if he knew their every move.

'Now go to the top of the stairs and watch me.' I went up and watched. He carried the pan, filled to the brim, steadily and surely— and at the top, not a ripple on the water.

'Wow' I said with admiration, 'You *are* fine.' And everything *was* fine. It was a happy home.

About that boiling water— there is always a cry for boiling water— not for boiling the baby! Hot water for a birth needed to be on hand in the bedroom, for hand washing and bathing the baby and washing the mother. In those days, many homes didn't have an upstairs bathroom, or a flat may have a shared bathroom. Bowls and buckets and saucepans of hot water, were the answer. It seems primitive now but we had to improvise many things. Many times a drawer was used for a crib and towels for blankets.

Most homes were simple by today's standards and had no central heating, few washing machines, terry nappies had to be boiled in any available pan or boiler. But critically there were few telephones. There was always a need to know the quickest route to get help if a mother had a post-natal bleed, or a baby failed to respond. Mothers were asked to keep a stock of pennies for the pay phone, and to know the route to the nearest phone box. I can't remember the blind father's arrangements for that but, it was obviously satisfactory.

And there *were* emergencies on the district when doctors were required. One night, when I was working in hospital, a call came for the 'Flying Squad.' The doctor who took the call, grabbed me and said 'Come with me.' She looked anxious.

We sped in the ambulance, blue lights flashing, to a block of nearby flats. The call had come from the fourth floor where apparently a woman had *'unexpectedly'* given birth and was haemorrhaging—bleeding. The door opened as we arrived and we entered a bedroom where a woman was lying in bed, with sheets and blankets up round her neck. A couple of men were in the room hovering.

'But where's the baby,' I asked.

'There,' and she pointed to the covers. I pulled back the sheets to find a new-born, still attached by the cord and looking very blue, lying in pools of blood under the covers.

'Quick, cut the cord,' the doctor gasped, 'I'll give her ergometrine.'

I cut the cord and tried to get the baby, to breathe. With hands shaking, the doctor gave the injection to stop the bleeding.

It didn't work at first, and tension rose, 'We going to lose her,' muttered the doctor. But finally, using various methods including massage, we managed to stop the flow.

The doctor set up an IV infusion and the patient was transferred to hospital, she nearly lost her life but both mother and baby survived. I don't know what was going on in that room; I suspect it may have been something criminal but don't know if it was taken any further.

I had many memorable experiences but one night stands out. My supervisor called me around 7pm to go and check a mother in labour. I went and as labour was advanced, stayed to deliver the baby. I needed to keep the supervisor informed, this meant trailing out to a public phone at regular intervals. I was so tired when I arrived home at midnight.

My mother was waiting. 'There's been a phone call and you've to go out again,' she told me, 'I'll make you a cup of tea—but you've no time to waste.'

I started to unpack my bag, 'I've got to clean this stuff and put it in the oven first.' I just wanted to go to bed.

Mum handed me some tea, 'Don't worry, I'll set the alarm and take it out in an hour.'

Once again, I went off on my bike. I stayed for the birth, going to the phone box to inform the midwife. I finished around 4am and went home.

Yet again my mother was waiting, 'She's just called,' she handed me an address, 'It's this woman and she said she's already checked her, but says there is enough time for you to go.'

Mum was annoyed, she thought I was being taken advantage of. My supervisor had checked the mother and decided it would wait until I got back, whilst she went off to bed. Exhausted I unpacked my bag, cleaned the instruments for sterilising and went off again as the sun was rising. Between all of these deliveries, there was a compulsory record to be made, detailing everything about the birth. All this took time.

After three deliveries in one long night, my supervisor said, 'We only have a short clinic this morning, so do that, then you can take the afternoon off.' Ready to start again that night!

My hospital colleagues envied me, I had more than one hundred deliveries on the district, whilst they could hardly complete the required number to qualify. Their midwives liked to do their own deliveries, whilst mine was lazy and left them all to me—on two districts. Most babies are born in the night hours; I wonder if she took pupils so she could stay in bed. Things have changed now.

36

SAILING AWAY ON THE QUEEN ELIZABETH

Finally, I had a chance to travel.

'You're going to America,' my friend squealed with envy, 'You are *so* lucky.'

'We're going in September, and we're sailing on the Queen Elizabeth. 'I was so excited, 'I just can't wait.'

When I told my mother she looked sad, she had lost so many of the people she loved. 'But we're only going for a year, maybe two—but we're *definitely* coming back.'

She held us lightly, never possessively, often saying, 'You have your own lives to live.' For that reason, it was easy to both go and also come back to her.

I knew we would come back from the USA—*and we did.* That is why it is included here. But first there were adventures ahead.

We were to be married in July 1961. Then we were off to Boston for a year where Colin had a Research Appointment at Massachusetts General Hospital.

When Mum was ironing my dress the night before the wedding, she said, 'This is one of the last things I will do for you.'

Again I said 'We are definitely coming back, you won't lose us and there will be lots of things I will need you to do!'

As she ironed the hem of the dress and I said, 'I'm so sorry about the table.'

'They are the marks of life—I shall treasure them.'

I made my own wedding dress from a beautiful white French material. It was heavy with a raised pattern and the hem was difficult to adjust.

Mary said, 'Stand on the table and I'll pin it up, put your shoes on though.' I climbed onto the table and she pinned it. 'Turn round,' and then, 'now back again.' All the time my stiletto heels, tap, tap, tapped into the table top.

Mum had recently bought a new oak Ercol dining suite, all the rage at the time. It was one of the first things they bought after the years of hardship. It was so new and now it was pock-marked by my heels. Mum, as always, said it was no use crying over spilt milk, what was done, was done. There were no recriminations, she knew how badly I felt.

'Don't worry, they are the marks of life, I shall treasure them and I will remember you.'

We married the next day and Mary and Ann were pretty bridesmaids with headdresses and bouquets of sweet peas. Dad had a close friend who was Events Manager at the Botanical Gardens in Edgbaston and he suggested we had our reception there. It was a day of glorious sunshine, the gardens were perfect for photographs and so were the hot houses with the pools and fountains. It was such a lovely place for a wedding.

Three weeks later Ann married and in one sense Mum lost two daughters in a month. Mary then announced that she was going to work in Bermuda. It was only in retrospect and with added maturity that I realise how traumatic it must have been. She didn't complain but it made me all the more determined to come back.

The trunk bought for the aborted Australian emigration and then used for Dunster holidays, was now packed for transit to the USA. Lovely red Cunard labels, 'not wanted on voyage' were stuck all over it. Vintage labels, reminders of past years, very desirable now.

We travelled third class–cabin class on the Queen Elizabeth 1, from Southampton to New York, a journey of six days at a cost of £60. We couldn't afford to fly; flights cost £80 each and were out of the question. At last I was travelling to those faraway places I so long had imagined and dreamed about.

We sailed on Sept 3, 1961. The ship was a quarter of a mile long with luxury shops and the usual lounges and restaurants, recliners on deck, a library, and a theatre. Our cabin, *one of many in third class, was deep down inside the ship*—a tiny room, without windows, about six-foot-wide by ten-foot-long with bunk beds. There was no ensuite . . .we shared a bathroom with the rest of the third class passengers. It didn't compare to today's luxury liners, but to us then, it was state of the art.

It was six days of luxury for those days. Sixteen years after the war, Britain's eating habits were still very conservative. But the dining room on the Queen Elizabeth was filled with delectable food—an amazing array as well as amazing amounts. Food we had never seen before, but normal today in cosmopolitan Britain. It was all new and exciting. . .from lifeboat drill to celebration dinners, to fabulous meals and massive choices.

Six days later we were up early to see the first sight of the Manhattan skyline as we sailed past the Statue of Liberty and down the Hudson river. The dock was heaving with people and we had to wait as luggage was unloaded. It took all day to disembark, to go through customs and have visas checked.

Eventually the friends who were meeting us with a 'U-Haul' trailer, found us, loaded the trunks, and we were off as the lights were coming on all over New York. Bright lights, flashing adverts and crowded streets pulsating with excitement.

And so we arrived for our new life and settled into new jobs. Colin at Massachusetts General Hospital and I got work at Harvard University in one of their research laboratories. My experience in the laboratories in Birmingham Medical School proved valuable.

The research in the department in Harvard was diverse and very cosmopolitan. Staff came from all over the world and one day I passed a young man in the corridor with sharp and intensely blue eyes. He nodded an English 'Good morning.'

I was with a friend and she said, 'You know who that is, don't you? ... It's Jim Watson who deciphered DNA, the genetic code.' She continued, 'Today he has heard that he has been awarded the Nobel Prize.'

The whole department celebrated.

We loved Boston from the start and fell in love with New England . . .

beautiful rolling countryside, pretty villages, white clap-board houses and steepled churches. Within weeks the 'Fall' brought clear hot days, brilliant blue skies and frosty nights which turned the maple trees red. Soon, vast swathes of rolling countryside were red and yellow, turning villages into picture postcard scenes. Stands of colourful Indian corn and massive pumpkins appeared by the roadside and on every veranda and step.

Fall in New England is the most incredible sight and brings 'leaf peepers' out on the trails year after year. It is also Mohawk Indian country and we drove the stunning Mohawk trail regularly. We return as often as we can for a visit.

We were only there for a year and the months rolled by so quickly. Winter and snow arrived and we skated outdoor on frozen ponds and rivers and spent weekends up in the mountains in Vermont and Maine. We shopped in amazing stores in Boston and on New York's fifth Avenue. Walked in Central Park and went to the top of the Empire State building– 102 floors– for incredible views over the City. We began to feel we didn't want to return. But we knew we must.

For as long as I could remember I wanted to travel and so had Colin. This was the opportunity. In the spring we bought a 1957 silver Chevrolet and planned a trip around America's National Parks— wish we had that car now. We took six weeks unpaid leave in June, and started off on an 11 thousand mile camping trip. We aimed to discover as much of America as possible. Our cherished '57 Chevy, was crammed with camping equipment including a tiny tent, sleeping bags, a stove, a suitcase of clothes and an icebox–a new invention in the sixties.

The roads in those days were quiet and empty. We meandered through Maryland, where the air was filled the perfume of honeysuckle and wild roses. Dawdled along the Skyline Drive in Virginia, with breathtaking vistas of blue mountains and old Colonial houses. Slept in isolated places under a canopy of stars and were scared in the night by the rustling and shuffling of raccoons and bears.

'Colin, what's that noise?' he was sound asleep, I dug him in the ribs, 'What's that noise?'

We opened the flap of the tent and peered out. 'It's a skunk, two skunks. . .aren't they beautiful.'

They were. Their black and white striped tails were right near the tent. We didn't dare move or make a sound, skunks look beautiful but spray a dreadful smell if disturbed.

'And look at that.'

There was an incredible display of magical fireflies, twinkling and dancing in the clear air around us. And cicadas chirped and sang or clicked like a band accompanying them. Cicadas can be heard all the way up the East coast of America.

We left the Blue Ridge Parkway at Roanoke to have the plugs and points changed on the car. While we waited, we went to a Virginian breakfast cafe.

It was self-serve with massive bars of every type of food. 'I'll have a full English,' said Colin, 'Look at that ham.' Thick slices of Virginia ham, fresh from the farm, was piled high on plates.

I think I had the same. 'Don't look now but I can't believe what the fellow behind has on his plate'.

'What?' Colin was dying to look.

'His plate is 18 inches long, at one end he has slices of ham, a mound of hash browns, two or three eggs, tomatoes then beans, then he has several pancakes covered in syrup, at the other end is a mound of strawberries and whipped cream.'

'Whew, no wonder he's so fat.'

He *was* huge but so were many of the others at the diner—a hazard of too many diner breakfasts!

Back on the mountain trail we headed down to the Smoky Mountains which were covered in the mists that gave them their name. In the mysterious interior we met 'Hill Billies' selling silver mountain craft and Cherokee Indians in full dress. Everywhere, we delayed and wanted to stay longer. Our far too big plan, was to reach the Canyons, explore San Francisco and Yosemite, travel the Pacific West Coast, visit Vancouver and return via Niagara. It sounds ridiculous to have planned so much, but our friends in Boston had already done the same.

But we dawdled and found we were behind schedule and so were determined not to stop in Mississippi—we would drive all day and night to catch up—so we thought.

37

MISSISSIPPI SUMMER NIGHT'S DREAM

I was looking at the map and wondering how we could speed up our journey. It was another thousand miles to San Francisco, that was only half way, and there was so much to see on the way. Should we drive all night? Heat shimmered on the road in the searing heat of the Mississippi summer afternoon. Overhead traffic lights on Route 45 blinked from red to green as we crossed an intersection into a small American town. Immediately, a white gloved policeman stepped from the curb into our path, signaling our car to pull over.

Nervously Colin whispered, 'What did I do? I was sure the lights were green'

'Can you step out of the car please?' We hastily got out; sure now that we were in some sort of trouble. We stood, looking hot and disheveled, and waited for the worst.

'Would you like a cool drink?' said the smiling policeman. Our mouths dropped as he continued, 'This is our hospitality week and we stop out of State cars and offer refreshments'.

A policeman with a gun was offering us a cold drink! We recovered enough to say 'Yes please' and noticed the overhead banner which said 'Booneville City of Hospitality'

Nearby a welcoming committee served fresh orange juice at a roadside booth, what a good idea; a short stop for the very welcome drink wouldn't harm. Little did we know.

We felt hot and sticky. There was no air conditioning in cars in those days and temperatures had soared into the nineties–over 32C. Colin had decided to grow a beard to save shaving, and so had a week of stubble. On top of that the American style of Bermuda shorts below the knees, made our *very short*, English shorts look embarrassingly unfashionable.

As we drank the ice cold fresh orange juice they wanted to know where we came from,

'You have such cute accents'.

I stopped myself saying 'We don't have accents—but *you* do'. There were lots of questions.

Eventually a distinguished looking lady asked, 'Would you like to be our guests for the night at the Town Motel?' We stared. . .what an odd thing to say.

She continued, 'Every year in hospitality week we invite an out of state couple to be our guests.'

Now we knew why they questioned us so intently. Two people 'out of State' but also from out of the country fitted their plan perfectly. We just didn't know what their plan was going to be.

'We really are in a hurry, we have to get on—but thank you so much.'

'But you have to stop somewhere for the night—its four o'clock—and our lovely town motel is right here.'

We felt pressurised, it was embarrassing—and it did seem a good chance to sleep in a bed and have a shower, and it would be free, in the end we agreed.

At that point our lady friend explained, 'There will be a banquet tonight and you will be the guests of honour.'

This was getting odder and odder. It really threw me. My mind started to race—I hadn't got evening wear in my camping clothes. I had one short cotton dress, would there be an iron in the motel?—I needed to wash my hair—I wished we had said no.

Eventually we found ourselves in a comfortable motel room wondering if we were dreaming. After the dreary heat and humidity of mid-afternoon we entered an oasis of cool. I found an iron, and Colin took his suit from the suitcase, and yes he really did take a suit on a camping trip! He had been told by friends to take a suit for when he went into a bank to get money. Times were so different. We showered and Colin shaved off his stubble.

The doorbell rang and I was handed a beautiful corsage of fresh white flowers to wear and a buttonhole for Colin. How relieved we were that he had brought that suit!

We were collected for the reception as the clear, black, Mississippi sky began to shimmer with a myriad stars. And what a reception. We stepped into a room of elegant ladies. Their dresses were long and fashionable, silk rustled, jewels flashed and each wore a large and elaborate corsage of flowers. We seemed to have stepped back in time into a different era. The Southern drawl, the lavish hospitality and the beautiful clothes seemed to belong to a more relaxed and slower age.

I felt so 'under-dressed'.

The charming Mayor of Booneville greeted us; a smiling little man dressed from top to toe in white, even down to white shoes and shiny white spats. The only relief was the black bootlace tie worn in a bow at the neck. Our hostesses were the Townswomen's Guild. Colin and the Mayor were the only men amongst a host of elegant ladies.

Mayor Marion took his seat at the top table, 'Colin, would you like to join me?'

The 1962 Beauty Queen sat on one side of Colin and her assistant on the other. I was ushered to a place at the side! However, I was feeling self-conscious in my cotton print dress, in spite of my own huge corsage, and was relieved to find myself off 'centre stage'. We enjoyed an excellent meal but at the end there was yet another surprise.

'Colin, it is the custom for the guest of honour to give a short speech,' said the Mayor, 'would you please speak a little on The British National Health Service!'

Colin wished he'd had time to prepare. However, he coped amazingly well and answered a barrage of questions from an audience that seemed puzzled by free British Health Care which was then in its fourteenth year.

As this came to an end – another request, 'And now Colin, tell us what you know about Communism in Britain.'

It was the era in America, under Jack Kennedy, of the Cuban crisis and of the fear of 'reds under the bed'—to use what was then a common expression. The questions continued about secret infiltration of communism in Britain. Colin probably knew less than they did and I guess our casual attitude seemed incomprehensible.

Eventually the evening ended and the Mayor presented Colin with a *large white plastic key with a thermometer in the centre*. . .Written on the key were the words, 'The Key to Booneville, Mississippi, City of Hospitality'.

It had been an unforgettable evening of Southern hospitality. But there was still more to come. As we thanked our new friends they said they wanted to take us on a tour of Booneville before we left.

Back in the Motel, we flopped onto our beds and laughed and giggled for ages. What a wonderful evening and what wonderful people. We really did love this country.

'I can't believe that just happened,' said Colin, 'They should have asked you about the NHS.'

'Did you see where they put me—away from sight and you with the beauty Queen.' More laughter, but were we just dreaming?. . . it could only happen in America.

The next morning was just as unusual as the first. We were taken around the town. First stop was a shoe factory where we were told to choose two pairs of shoes each. The next manufactured shirts and blouses and we were told to choose whatever we wanted. In keeping with the events of the last few hours the morning felt surreal.

Finally, back on route 45 we wondered, 'Did that really happen?'. . .'And why to us?' Nothing in this apparently featureless town had been quite what it seemed. Time seemed to have stood still. *In all the days and adventures that followed Booneville was truly unique.*

Our Mississippi interlude eventually became a cherished memory, and a story we would recount over and over in the years to come. The white plastic key still hangs on the wall as a reminder of a time gone but frequently remembered.

We wouldn't have missed Booneville, but there was a little more than four weeks left to do the rest of our trip. It was a thousand miles to San Francisco and on the way we wanted to stop in many places. This time we really did drive all day and part of the night. But we still stopped and marvelled at the ancient cliff dwellings of Mesa Verde. . .were 'wowed' by the exotic rock formations in Bryce Canyon. . .and completely stunned by the grandeur of the Grand Canyon. That was amazing, beyond expectation.

Aware of the passing time, we still couldn't miss Las Vegas. The 'strip' in those days was just that—*one* road with brightly lit casinos and shabby motels. A shabby motel was our home for a night. Everything was chained to the wall—bed, table, chair and mirror. A notice declared, '*You can remove anything that is not chained for a souvenir.*'—that was just an ash tray.

From there we drove through Death Valley, the lowest, hottest, driest place on earth in our car without air conditioning. Even the air coming through the window was hot.

'Colin, I can't cope with this heat.'

'There's nowhere to stop, why don't you get ice out of the ice-box, wrap it in a cloth and hold it.'

So I did, taking turns to hold it to my head and then Colin's as he drove. With relief we reached Yosemite National Park where it was cool and pleasant. In fact, we camped above the snow-line in bear country and saw bears and their cubs. This was an incredible place and we could have spent the whole time there.

At last we arrived in San Francisco—time to put the suit on and go to a bank. So many things to see and do and no time to write about them here.

From San Francisco we drove through the Sequoia National Park where the great Redwood trees reach the sky and the tops can't be seen. And then up the West Coast to Vancouver Island. Another thousand miles, with National Parks on the way. By now we had climbed mountains, crossed several deserts and seen amazing scenery in this incredible country.

On Vancouver Island we stayed with my family who sent the magazines in wartime that first made me want to travel. A family reunion.

'Don't you look like your Father. . .and you must be my cousin. . .you look just like Elaine in England. . .I can't believe it. . .We're so glad you came. . .We'll have a party.'

Vancouver Island is surrounded by water, with mountains, rainforests, beaches, rivers and lakes and has a diverse multitude of wildlife. This beautiful setting is complemented by lovely towns and settlements. No wonder my Aunt and Uncle emigrated in the 1920s.

One fun day we went high up into the interior to a logging camp where my cousin was the Supervisor. Here we watched the fascinating process of felling trees and transporting the logs by river to town. We didn't want to leave. A few days later we crossed back into the States to visit the Seattle World Fair and then drove to Calgary where the stampede had just begun. We watched the rodeo and saw the cowboys and the bucking broncos.

We stood and watched the procession, then Colin said, 'Look who's coming in this car.'

Cowboy film stars, Dale Evans and Roy Rogers drove past in an extended white Cadillac to the cheers of the crowd. More cheers for Indians in full dress and feathers who rode bareback through the streets of this *small* town.

Since then, this small town found oil and became a *big* town—one of the largest in Canada with sky scrapers and a multi-million-dollar oil business. Between all these places we stopped and camped in National Parks, the largest and most amazing being Yellowstone with boiling mud pots, spouting geysers, moose and bears and rumbling volcanoes.

The last two thousand miles we did in three days, travelling day and night. Finally we reached the amazing Niagara Falls and then back to Boston. . .we made it all the way. This last page has taken a few minutes to write but took weeks to travel and that was much too fast in this vast and beautiful country.

38

BACK HOME TO BIRMINGHAM

We stayed on in Boston for another Fall, reluctant to leave the country we loved so much. But we finally sailed back to England in December 1962. We left crisp, clear skies of winter sunshine and arrived in Southampton in fog. The whole country was blanketed in wet damp white, thick, thick fog. Dad and my brother-in-law came to meet us. We saw them shivering on the dockside as we disembarked.

'At last, you're back,' Dad hugged me. It was so good to see him again and I realised how much I missed them. 'We've had a terrible journey,' he said, 'we started out at four this morning because of the fog.'

I handed him a tiny bundle, 'Here's your present from Boston Dad.'

He was overjoyed as he took his first grandchild, 'Isn't he lovely, hello Mark, I'm your Grandad'

Mark was just eight weeks old and a perfect reminder of a wonderful time in our lives. After a slow foggy journey, we arrived home in Birmingham. It was so good to be back and good to be home.

'I told you we'd come back'. . .I handed Mum her Grandson and she immediately took over, thrilled to have a baby to fuss over. And I was a child at home again. There were so many stories to tell and experiences to share and it took days, some stories we are still telling.

A Birmingham child returned.

ABOUT THE AUTHOR

Muriel Bolton grew up in Birmingham but has lived for many years in Bristol with her husband, a retired University Lecturer. They have a son and two daughters who left for University and then returned to settle Between them they have provided nine grandchildren and this has meant lots of fun-filled family celebrations over the years.

Muriel trained as a nurse and midwife and then later as a Counsellor. She loves travelling, all the creative arts and enjoys writing but this is the first book she has written.

Printed in Great Britain
by Amazon

22816618R00119